Michael Hopkins

Cristina Donati

Michael Hopkins

SKIRA

Editor
Luca Molinari

Art Director
Marcello Francone

Editing
Francesca Malerba&Martine Buysschaert

Layout
Paola Ranzini

Translations
Anne Ellis Ruzzante, David Stanton

First published in Italy in 2006 by
Skira Editore S.p.A.
Palazzo Casati Stampa
via Torino 61
20123 Milano
Italy
www.skira.net

© 2006 by Skira editore

Printed and bound in Italy, September 2006
First edition

ISBN 10 88-7624-653-3
ISBN 13 978-88-7624-653-1

Distributed in North America by Rizzoli
International Publications, Inc., 300 Park
Avenue South, New York, NY 10010.
Distributed elsewhere in the world by
Thames and Hudson Ltd., 181a High
Holborn, London WC1V 7QX, United
Kingdom.

Cover
Hopkins Studio, Marylebone, London,
1984;
detail of the fabric tensile structure
photo Richard Davies

Front cover flap
Glyndebourne Opera House, Sussex,
1994
photo Richard Davies

Back cover flap
Hopkins House, London, 1976
photo Matthew Wienreb

p. 10
Constructing the Patera components
with a high degree of accurancy

p. 24
Detail of a Patera unit, London, 1985

p. 62
Bracken House, London, 1992

p. 106
The Wellcome Trust Gibbs Building,
London, 2004

p. 260
Model view of Pisa headquarters, 2003

I would like to thank Sir Michael and
Lady Hopkins for their fundamental
support and the Hopkins Studio for
their collaboration. Special thanks
goes to Alet Mans for her assistance in
researching the iconographic material

Contents

A generation separates the two icons of the modernity that mark the beginning and the maturity of Sir Michael Hopkins's architectural career: two works that symbolically start and consolidate a long cycle of experimentation, apparently without a leitmotif, but, on the contrary, inspired by a profound sense of continuity.

In 1976 Hopkins applied industrial technology to a house consisting of a "skeleton" and "skin" that challenged the limits of dematerialized construction: this is the Hopkins House, a pure and transparent volume inserted in an elegant conservative street in the Hampstead area of London. In 2000, next to the Palace of Westminster, he completed Portcullis House, the new Parliamentary Building, where he employed an innovative technique of reinforced stone construction.

His formative years, spent discovering old buildings in the beautiful Dorset countryside, were followed by the period of training at the Architectural Association, where the debate on the avant-garde movement was in full swing. His collaboration with Norman Foster, his interest in Richard Buckminster Fuller's utopias, and his admiration for the experimental works of Charles and Ray Eames paved the way for his industrial mannerist phase: this was the period of the beginning of information technology and the radical High-Tech, that was inexorably transformed into a crisis of conscience.

At the beginning of the 1990s, influenced perhaps by the approach of the new millennium, Hopkins began to elaborate a historical synthesis. His architecture took a great step forward, inaugurating the "Third Machine Age" – an era in which technology was no longer at the service of progress for its own sake, but rather for man and the safeguarding of our planet. The challenge of sustainable building stimulated Hopkins to undertake a process of updating traditional materials, to which he transferred the know-how acquired in the sector of the light weight construction. This renewed interest in history, in which he sought to wed sustainability to the material aesthetic, resulted in his being awarded the prestigious gold medal of the Royal Institute of British Architects in 1994. This was the high point of a working life focused on comprehending the language of the Modern Movement: from its radical phase to its maturity, Hopkins proposed a new reading of modernity, confirming his position as a leading figure in the contemporary world.

Tradition and Metamorphosis of Architecture in the Third Machine Age: phases of a work in progress

From Dorset to Radical Experimentation

Michael Hopkins is often described as the most British of the architects on the international scene: this Britishness is not easy to define because it is the result of a cultural legacy that extends beyond the professional sphere to the autobiographical one. A builder's son, Hopkins attended Sherbourne School and, at the age of seventeen, enrolled in the Bournemouth Art School: bored by the official courses, he preferred to pursue his interest in architecture taking long bicycle rides in the Dorset countryside, where the landscape links architecture and the environment in mutual harmony. Small churches, cottages and country houses aroused Hopkins's interest, and he discovered the link between the built environment and nature through an analysis of these buildings, with their vernacular but authentic taste. These flights from the monotony of formal education were the first signs of a concept of architecture that, although not yet realizable, formed the germ of the Britishness that was to characterize the succinct and contextual approach of his mature works.

After a year and a half, Hopkins interrupted his studies in order to work as a trainee for local architects and subsequently in London, where he worked in the offices of Frederick Gibberd and Basil Spence. His passion for architecture was now sufficiently strong to encourage him to recommence his studies: he enrolled as a second year student at the Architectural Association in London, considered the best school in the country, where he began his long journey through the world of architecture and contemporary construction.

At the beginning of the 1960s the prestigious London school was an alternative institution where culture, experimentation, and futurology inspired the teaching of such illustrious lecturers as Cedric Price, Bob Maxwell, John Winter, Alan Colquhoun, and Peter Smithson. Aesthetics and the style of the architecture were secondary, almost irrelevant aspects; the teaching stressed the importance of place – the context, consisting of the social composition, density of population, relationships and links, were considered more important parameters than the world of construction or knowledge of materials. Le Corbusier, Alvar Aalto, and Ralph Erskine were presented as the true masters of the Modern Movement because their poetic purpose went beyond the definition and communication of a style.

After graduating in 1963, Hopkins worked with Leonard Manasseh on the design of new halls of residence for Leicester University and subsequently with Tom Hancock on the master plan for the expansion of Peterborough (a residential area for 100,000 inhabitants). Meanwhile his father had become Director of a national Construction firm, and he was

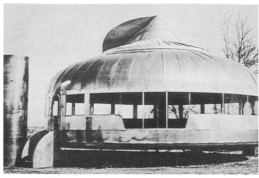

able to obtain an interesting commission in 1968: the planning of an industrial estate in Goole, Yorkshire. It was in this period that Team 4 – a group of architects comprising Norman and Wendy Foster and Richard and Su Rogers – broke up; thus Foster was looking for work, while Hopkins was seeking an expert partner. They worked together for the next seven years.

The Goole project never got off the drawing board, but Hopkins and Foster found they shared the same passion for a concept of architecture inspired by the philosophy of such leading figures as Raphael Soriano and Craig Ellwood, and the methods of Charles and Ray Eames and the West Coast School.

A subsequent commission had a more fortunate outcome, and a critical success that was of vital importance for the development of the careers of the two architects and for their approach to their work in the following years. Philip Dowson, a founder partner of Arup Associates, suggested that Foster design the IBM offices at Cosham; the project was for a temporary building for 750 employees while their new offices were being built in Portsmouth. This was an ideal commission for putting their technological theories into practice. The scheme required an economical and adaptable building that could be assembled rapidly: the solution was an elegant, light envelope supported by a structure of slender columns and rectangular beams, clad with a glass skin enclosing a deep, flexible air-conditioned space. This was a building system that strongly echoed the American practice, but was still new to Britain.

The Cosham project marked the beginning of the adventure that was to absorb Hopkins's creativity for the next ten years, as he pursued the dream of architecture as an industrial product, of "architecture or revolution" in the words of Le Corbusier, who urged architects to emerge from their eclectic torpor in order to participate with a fresh spirit in building the world from scratch.

Around the middle of the 1940s, the American engineer and inventor Richard Buckminster Fuller applied industrial technology to the building sector and created the Wichita House, a mass-producible home that never got beyond the prototype stage, even if, at least in theory, two hundred could be produced every day. Despite this, the utopian dream of transforming architecture into a refined industrial product was now close to realization.

Charles and Ray Eames,
Eames House,
Santa Monica, 1949

Richard Buckminster Fuller,
Wichita House prototype,
1946

In 1976 Hopkins founded his practice – Michael Hopkins and Partners – with the aim of continuing along the path he had already taken, giving concrete form to experiments he already carried out with prototypes. The first building the new practice completed was the house-cum-office that Hopkins built, together with his wife, Patty, in Hampstead, one of London's most exclusive residential areas. An elegant row of villas in Neo-Georgian style is interrupted by an extremely light, glazed volume that has become part of the history of architecture, as one of the icons of the radical growth of the Modern Movement. This open-plan glass house and its dematerializing effect is the expression of the "tectonic annulment" that induced Buckminster Fuller to ask the Hopkins how much their house weighed.

The Hopkins House is the demonstration that results achieved together with Norman Foster with the industrial building types could be transferred to dwellings. It was in this spirit that Hopkins formulated the radical epilogue to Le Corbusier's thought and inaugurated the second phase of the Modern Movement and the early period of High Tech. In this phase, still pursuing the idea of the building as a product, he completed some of his most outstanding examples of industrial architecture, such as the Greene King Brewery Depot (1977–80), the Patera Building System (1980–82), the Schlumberger Cambridge Research Centre (1982–92) and the Solid State Logic factory (1986–88).

This first cycle of designs, which could be described as "structural radicalism", was characterized by the renewal of traditional building techniques, and culminated in the use of technological processes and components that had been developed in fields other than the building industry, especially sectors like aerospace, which seemed to produce more precise results. Thus, with the ambitious aim of transforming buildings into industrial products, the "machine aesthetic" was born, inspired by the cultural climate described by Reyner Banham in his book *Theory and Design in the First Machine Age* (1960). Banham's technology is a discipline that initiates a profound change capable of interrupting the process of stylistic renewal: "architecture now makes a break with tradition. It must perforce make a fresh start".

The characteristics of the projects of Hopkins's early period are expressions of compositional logic based on serial repetition, linearity of form, flexibility of the plan, and dematerialization of the volume. These are buildings composed of "kits of parts" to be assembled, taken down and reassembled elsewhere: objects without a genius loci, they are laconic, immaterial machines that may be located anywhere and come to life when their lights are turned on, communicating their internal vibrancy to the neighborhood. A light skin and a filigree of cables enclose a space that has lost its plastic value in order to be replaced by the representation of its function. High Tech is, therefore, the extreme form of functionalist architecture. Function overcomes the need to model space and function is allowed to express itself without space having to interpret it or give it a form. Louis Sullivan's old maxim, "form follows function", is no longer applicable: function itself becomes poetry, kinetic poetry, movement, and three-dimensional dynamism for architecture that no longer needs to conceal its contents from the world.

At the beginning of the 1990s, transparent architecture i.e. steel and glass construction had reached a high level of expertise, it was no longer a challenge, it had become a game conducted as an aesthetic spectacle for which, however, unexpected epilogues were predicted. Banham had already warned that what we have hitherto understood as architecture, and what we are beginning to understand of technology may be incompatible disciplines.

Just as Gothic structuralism thrust flying buttresses further and further towards the sky – towards the infinite, the immaterial, the spiritual and the sacred – until the structure risked collapsing, so the radical structuralism of the twentieth century eliminated both the beaux arts composition and the concept of mass in architecture, as enunciated by the Modern Movement, in order to propose a language for envisaging the future that did not, however, affirm the reality of the political systems or socio-economic logistics. On the contrary, the idea of positive progress that liberates man from the slavery of the laws of nature seemed suddenly to turn against humankind itself: the planet fell sick, the economy entered a period of recession and architecture faced a serious identity crisis.

Buckminster Fuller's Wichita House – originally the Dymaxion House, which he described as "a machine for living in" – never managed to become part of the industrial chain, nor did it ever change the dynamics of the world. When the exponents of the British Structuralist school – Michael Hopkins, Norman Foster, Richard Rogers and Nicholas Grimshaw – weighed up the first ten years of their activity, they were conscious that some of them had hardly ever had the opportunity to build in their homeland and others, such as Hopkins, had not had the opportunity to realise the utopia of the avant-garde period: the buildings of the early period were the expression of a hyper-functionalism that transformed them into sophisticated one-offs.

How, therefore, can we define High Tech: as a movement, avant-garde or otherwise, or a phenomenon? High Tech is a journalistic expression of American origin referring to what is in effect the most radical form of the Modern Movement. It is curious to note that it was Britain, which had been so reluctant to assimilate the Rationalist ideology, that produced its most extreme manifestation. Is High Tech, therefore, the epilogue or a posthumous avant-garde of the Modern Movement?

It could be pointed out that first High-Tech architecture was a new direction in a British context of the Bauhaus philosophy; the British Structuralist school, apparently devoid of historical association, had its roots in pragmatism tending towards the poetics of building that in the nineteenth century generated such masterpieces as Joseph Paxton's Crystal Palace (1851). This tendency to challenge the limits of technology has long been present in Britain: for instance in the construction of iron bridges, such as the pioneering one at Ironbridge, near Coalbrookdale in Shropshire (1779), the first High-Tech structure in history.

Thus, this is a culture that identifies itself neither with the German aesthetic philosophy, regarded as too sophisticated, nor with the stylistic reduction of the American type as advocated by Philip Johnson or Henry-Russell Hitchcock. High Tech is, therefore, a posthumous autochthonous re-elaboration of the Modern Movement that was historically and culturally more suited to the British sensibility, enriching the vision of the Città Nuova of the Italian Futurists, firstly with the fantastic images of Buckminster Fuller's utopias and then with the Archigram's designs.

Towards the end of the twentieth century architecture faced its first profound crisis of conscience and the four exponents of British Structuralism focused on their own personal growth: Richard Rogers had a messianic interest in the city, while Norman Foster's great passion for the future led him to design buildings apparently devoid of structural elements where the spaces are ideal settings for the protagonists of Isaac Asimov's novels. Hopkins neither disavows the future nor forgets the past, but, seeking to come to terms with history, he tackles the projects of his mature period with a lucid synthesis of memory and technology. In fact, "Technology Comes to Town" was the title of a lecture that Hopkins gave in 1992 to the Royal Society of Arts in London, when he set forth the principles on which his new architecture is founded. When technology comes to town, the results are indeed surprising.

High Tech and Continuity
In 1990 Martin Pawley wrote *Theory and Design in the Second Machine Age*: this book marks the end of an era and the dawn of a new approach to architecture dominated by the affirmation of information technology in a world where instability was the norm. Technology transfer aiming at developing new design based on industrialization and high performance construction processes did not constitute a full response to the dynamics of a changing world heading to the complexity of globalization. These changes in the development of the political systems are reflected by new pressures on architecture; as a result Hopkins progressively widened his field of interest from the constructive detail and the building to architecture in its context and the contradictory and fascinating organism that is the city. Thus, from his research into materials, his experimentation with construction and the building site, Hopkins progressed to the complex notion of architecture as space, form and urban interaction. The opportunity for this arose with his commission for Mound Stand for Lord's Cricket Ground in Marylebone, London where it became inevitable that he would have to deal with the unfinished brick arcade designed in the 1890s by Frank Verity, which Hopkins went on to complete.

The force of history – and also of the tradition of a sport, cricket, that is the very symbol of Englishness – required him to take a very definite position. The new building represented a turning-point, new awareness, a step forward: but in which direction? This was the period when critics set their seal on the already advanced crumbling of consensus on modern architecture, when Prince Charles exhorted architects to abandon false progress in favour of the styles of the past, and when there was a trend towards economic recession that caused deep cultural disorientation and an identity crisis strengthened by the power of the anti-modernist lobby. No alternative could, however, ignore a critical analysis of the contemporary condition and a laborious examination of the past: should this involve a reappraisal of tradition, perhaps also a return to classicism, or did it mean going back to the historicist irony of Post-Modernism? The radical, industrial, and mannerist High Tech that Colin Davis described in his important book published in this period, was already on the decline, threatened by the spread of the intellectual thought that heralded the end of the millennium which urged that this event should be accompanied by radical developments in architecture.

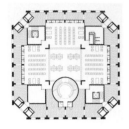

Louis Kahn, Phillips Exeter Academy, New Hampshire, 1965-72

Thus Hopkins accepted the challenge posed by the crisis of the Modern Movement, left unresolved by both Post-Modernism and the plethora of "isms" that sped like meteors across the firmament of architecture in the 1980s and 1990s. Casting his gaze back in time, and accepting no compromises, Hopkins sought continuity that did not speak the language of the styles. Without seeking to imitate the aesthetic values of the past, he delved into the ethical sense of the spirit of history. He wanted to start afresh with wider perspectives allowing the creation of the synthesis that had been denied to architecture that broke with the past: the expression of a new youthful, fundamentalist spirit. The *tabula rasa* approach no longer provided an adequate answer to the intellectual and formal questions of the late twentieth century. The only solution was a difficult confrontation with memory that had to be reassessed without attempting to revive earlier styles but with a view to the renewal of technology, materials and the language of form.

Hopkins dwelt on the emotions he had experienced and explored his emotive knowledge of the architecture of the Dorset countryside that he had acquired when still a student; he read again J.M. Richard's texts on functionalist architecture and Eric De Maré's photographic books focusing on the disturbing poetry of the early industrial buildings of the nineteenth century. The historic comprehension gave birth to the new architecture rooted in the purism of John Ruskin and Augustus Pugin, and their respect for the honesty of materials: stone, wood, brick, concrete and copper became new materials, the formal and constructional potential of which had to be explored with the necessary modern orthodoxy. Hopkins described the Lord's Cricket Ground Mound Stand project as his own personal "reconciliation with history" and with the city, substantiated in a work that tells the story of technology from the pragmatism of the Victorian Age to Buckminster Fuller's "ephemeralization" doing ever more with ever less: this is a story that, surprisingly, appears to be devoid of conflicts. Verity's arcade was rebuilt and completed, but not merely with a view to its restoration: the heavy brick structure engages in a dialogue with the lighter technology of steel and glass and the network of cables supporting the fabric membrane roof covering the building with an elegant sense of continuity. Hopkins discovered, in fact, that he shared Verity's passion for materials and construction: this continuity formed the basis for a new tectonic reflecting the growth of the techno-industrial ideology of the early High Tech and the new form of the Modern

Movement. The architecture of the Mound Stand is a synthesis of Victorian pragmatism, the rigour of the Bauhaus and High-Tech euphoria.

Just as he had understood and respected Verity's thought, Hopkins modernized Sir Albert Richardson's architecture when he rebuilt Bracken House, the former Financial Times building occupying a whole block close to St Paul's Cathedral in the heart of the City of London. Once again Hopkins was confronted with an urban context and the renovation of a portion of the pre-existing building. A theme that he had already tackled at Lord's, he investigated it further in Richardson's building, where historical analysis revealed echoes of Italian Baroque. He combined its classicism with High Tech and British Structuralism to produce a design that John Winter described as "one of the most creative developments on the British architectural scene". The preservation of the wings, with the new oval block between them, was a courageous solution that avoids the historicist approach by creating a totally new compositional synthesis. The main elevation, divided up by the bronze columns of the load-bearing structure and the bay windows, recalls Peter Ellis's Oriel Chambers built in Liverpool in 1864. This is not a citation, but rather a language that is renewed in order to create an innovative load-bearing façade with its powerful rhythm: the stone base supports the brackets onto which the bronze columns, attached to the beams along the edges of the floor slabs, discharge their load. This is constructional tour de force, the meaning of which was thus explained by Hopkins himself: "If what you construct is what you end up seeing, there is a chance that you get some quality in your architecture".

The commission for the Glyndebourne Opera House confirmed the new relationship between technology and context that became the theoretical and methodical basis for a fresh approach to architecture.

Mies van der Rohe, Crown Hall, Chicago, 1956

Glyndebourne wedded the craftsman's skills to high technology and established Hopkins's interest in introducing innovative techniques in the use of traditional materials.

Designed in the same period as Bedfont Lakes, Glyndebourne, although very different, had the same structural concept: the brick piers at Glyndebourne taper upwards like the steel columns at Bedfont Lakes, a similar expression of a reducing load applied to different building materials. This is a construction and aesthetic strategy that the architect continued to investigate in the projects for the Inland Revenue Centre in Nottingham and the Queen's Building in Cambridge. Thus Hopkins became the "acceptable face of Modernism": the British Establishment, traditionally hostile to modernity, recognized the value of his architecture, so that in the 1990s he received the Royal Institute of British Architects gold medal and a knighthood.

From the manneristic industrial architecture of his earlier designs, Hopkins proceeded to his mature period, when he believed, to paraphrase Louis Sullivan's adage, that "form follows materials", interpreting this in two different ways: light suspended structures and heavy prefabricated elements. He elaborated his own version of architectural technology that addressed such major themes as monumentality and history, the centrality of the plan and symmetry, truth to materials, technological innovation, environmental compatibility and energy conservation.

Buildings such as the Inland Revenue Centre in Nottingham (1992–95), the Queen's Building in Cambridge (1993–95), the Wildscreen interactive museum in Bristol (1995–2000), the Jubilee Campus of Nottingham University (1996–99), and the New Parliamentary Building in London (1989–2000) are typical of Hopkins's mature period, demonstrating how innovation has allowed traditional building methods to evolve while respecting the environment and the British cultural traditions. The structural system, with unreinforced brick piers, adopted for the elevations of the Inland Revenue Centre is, therefore, of particular importance both for its compositional value and for its contribution to the innovation of building processes: the prefabrication of the brick piers in a factory ensured great precision, safety and speed of assembly on site. The New Parliamentary Building expresses unexpected potentialities of stone, which assumes unexpected lightness reminiscent of the nearby Gothic Palace of Westminster. Thus Hopkins invented "High-Tech stone and brick", and, taking account of limited resources, transformed sustainability into a discipline that updated the language of Traditional materials.

The Germanic rigor of Mies van der Rohe's architecture, Louis Kahn's vision of history of composition, and British functionalism stimulated reflection and analysis. A notable example is the composition with tapered piers and flat arches of Kahn's Phillips Exeter Academy Library, New Hampshire (1972), which Hopkins adapted on a number of occasions, with a continually evolving use of technology. The renewal of the language of the materials is a commitment that Hopkins shared with Kahn, like the aspiration to resolve the schemes with a single succinct and legible gesture revealed in the preparation of simple symmetric plans, almost dia-

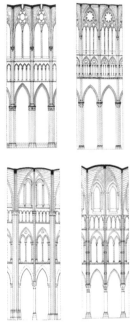

Examples of Gothic naves
Rheims cathedral,
from 1211
Amiens cathedral,
from 1220
Noyon cathedral,
1170-1185
Laon cathedral,
from 1170

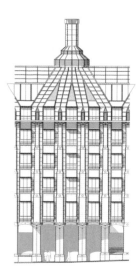

The new Parliamentary Building seen from the courtyard

grammatic, as if seeking an archetypal form, the expression of the synthesis of the problem. The clarity of the plans and legibility of the structure establish the criteria and dimensions of the composition; variation for its own sake is rejected, because architecture is not a "visual art" but rather the "art of building"; thus, the design and details require continuous perfecting.

Hopkins is a Rationalist Structuralist who reinterprets Schinkelian classicism in a Miesian spirit: this is classicism rooted in the logic of construction, not that of aesthetics or form. In Hopkins's architecture there is, however, a formal value to be found in the repetition of components and in the insistence on details that are increasingly perfected, until they themselves become a stylistic language. Morphemes of this grammar are the elements forming the "kit of parts" of the building, in accordance with the High-Tech tenets that have always constituted the basis of Hopkins's architectural philosophy. They are evidence of the coherence and intellectual continuity to be found in the perfection of such elements as the tapered piers, flat arches, glass-block vertical circulation towers, curved floor slabs made of fair-faced concrete, lead roofs and fabric tensile structures covering a central area of the complex, such as, a foyer, an entrance or a space for socialization. These eye-catching, fantastic structures contrast with the solidity of their bases: the membrane structure is architecture in tension; masonry is architecture in compression.

Bioclimatics is a new development that is having a profound effect on the way architects go about the design of buildings; it is, in fact, a new commitment that is transforming Hopkins from a Rationalist Structuralist to a Rationalist Environmentalist. Sustainable building has had an enormous influence on his architecture: the outline of the chimneys of the New Parliamentary Building, the glass-block towers of the Inland Revenue Centre, the curved structure of the roofs of the Evelina Children's Hospital and the Wellcome Trust Gibbs Building. Projects nearing conclusion, such as the business centre in Dubai, the research centre at Yale and the towers in Tokyo, demonstrate that Hopkins's new architecture is also celebrated outside Britain.

Once again Hopkins, who was the first architect to combine heavy construction with the light weight construction of steel and glass, was also the first to amalgamate sustainability with aesthetics in order to meet the demands of a sick planet. So what direction are the practice's new projects taking?

The epoch-making transition to the architecture of the third millennium has been sanctioned by the awareness that tradition can be neither a fetish nor a panacea in which to take refuge, that progress must not constitute a break with the past, as the masters of the early Modernism ingenuously proclaimed, and that architecture follows a path studded with traumas, failures, innovations and recurrences. This is a dynamic line of thought in which there is ethical continuity linking past, present and future. Because it necessarily lasts a long time, architecture can express, more than any other art form, this sense of continuity. Hopkins's architecture, on the other hand, expresses the desire to communicate a time-less ethic – in architecture, tradition and modernity are only metacate-gories of the limited human memory.

Towards a Definition of the Sustainable Community
The twentieth century was a period that began with a metamorphosis, the avant-garde, faith in the future and radical progress; it then slid in-to a form of introspection, of historicist psychoanalysis that caused it to withdraw into itself, so that it even denied the value of its achievements. Modern architecture,described by Reyner Banham as that of the "First Machine Age", progressed rapidly, inebriated by the discovery of a new pow-er: that of technology. "Man multiplied by the motor" – to use a famous phrase of the founder of the Futurism, Filippo Tommaso Marinetti – was different from the man on horseback who had dominated the world since its origins: he was a man who dreamed of building a new mechanized world where a totally new aesthetic would hold sway.

In 1914 Antonio Sant'Elia wrote the manifesto describing these changes in the human spirit: "We must invent and construct afresh the modern city, which will become an immense building site every part of which is tumultuous, active, mobile and dynamic, and the modern house will be like a gigantic machine. Lifts must not be hidden away like tapeworms in the stairwells, but they must climb, like iron and glass snakes, along the façades. The house of concrete, glass and iron, unpainted and with-out sculpture, rich only in the beauty deriving from its lines and forms, extraordinarily brutal in its mechanical simplicity, as high and as broad as necessary, not as laid down in the town planning regulations, must rise on the brink of a tumultuous abyss".

Observing many High-Tech works of the radical period, one is aware of the degree to which early British structuralism has interpreted the philosophical thought of the Modernism of the Italian Futurists. The ide-ological enthusiasm of the earlier part of the twentieth century was ex-tinguished by the sense of bewilderment prevailing at the end of the century: on the threshold of the third millennium, architecture was in a dire state, strangled as it was by environmental disasters, the strug-gle for power between the colossi of the economy, standardized global thought and an ever-weaker historical and cultural legacy. In a situa-tion in which progress seems to be the main culprit for the failure of the built world, it is easy to take the path of historical nostalgia, ideal-ization and ideologization of the past and memory, as if time could be handled like a Moviola.

Towards the end of the 1990s the world of architecture was once again divided into passéists and futurists, repeating in a worse way what had already taken place at the beginning of the twentieth century: crit-ics were polarized between those who still believed in progress as un-remitting global renewal and those who were no longer able to see the possibility of further growth and sought refuge in historical nostalgia. It was in this period that Hopkins proposed the third alternative: the in-novation of memory.

Glyndebourne Opera House, 1989-94

Wellcome Trust Building, London, 1999–2004

New Square, Bedfont Lakes, London, 1989–92

This solution was not that of the stylistic renewal advocated by the various tendencies that journalists amused themselves by labelling with engaging isms, but rather that of technological developments that were to improve the performance of materials in order to create innovative forms and a new aesthetic. Paraphrasing Kenneth Frampton, Hopkins rediscovered the "poetics of construction" through "new tectonics" that had their roots in the reinterpretation of all the materials, traditional and modern, that were an expression of the logic of the High-Tech credo. Thus wood, brick and stone are transformed into precision materials to be assembled on site or prefabricated in a factory with the same logic that is applied to the light weight construction of steel and glass. The juxtaposition of technologies highlights the evolution of the performance of a traditional material like brick, which can now be used in perfect harmony with the most recent construction processes.

Thus, Hopkins went beyond his own time and started the "Third Machine Age" in which technology is a tool that has evolved in the sure hands of an architect who has settled the conflict between the built work and nature. Technology is no longer a means for guiding progress, but a science in harmony with the environment: the themes of sustainable building are at the centre of Hopkins's present work, which restores to architecture its historic growth and concord with the entire ecosystem. This new awareness transforms architecture into a category of ethics, a global discipline able to respond to the emergency facing our planet.

The construction, management and maintenance of buildings produce almost 50 per cent of the carbon dioxide emissions in the United Kingdom: this is a figure that cannot but provoke the need to respond with targeted reduction strategies. Hopkins's present work is thus aimed at establishing a method that can transform the structure into a composition able to interact with the building's ventilation system: thus the materials and their aesthetic logic – from dimensioning to the assembly techniques – contribute to producing energy with the final objective of reaching self-sufficiency entirely based on systems of passive production.

In a recent publication (The Energy Review, 2002), the British government stressed that by 2050 the nation should be able to reduce carbon emissions by 60 per cent in order to ensure climatic stability and that responsibility for 51 per cent of this reduction lay with the building industry. There is no doubt that a target of 60 per cent is still hypothetical, but it is, nevertheless, a factor that has to be taken into account when reflecting on the significance of the sustainable programmes. Hopkins's bioclimatic philosophy is a global vision of construction: in other words, it is not sufficient to add systems for passive energy production to a building that is not in harmony with the environment or is user-unfriendly. Sustainability is, therefore, a holistic discipline that combines architecture with engineering and the environment: environmental compatibility and energy conservation are two faces of the same coin, and their correct interpretation allows a notable saving in the management and maintenance costs of a building, and greater sense of well-being for its users. Sustainability is a concept of construction that, as in antiquity, puts the human being in the centre. Hopkins's recent works comprise a series of strategies aimed at bringing the environment closer to the building: the form and the orientation of the building creates a controlled microclimate; adequate thermal mass and nocturnal cooling techniques of the structure; integrated solar screening; reduced width of buildings in order to improve natural ventilation and illumination; wind turbines; ventilation by the "chimney effect" (drawing of warm air upwards); glass with a high thermal insulating capacity; photovoltaic cells; thermal wheels; solar chimneys; high-performance insulating panels; atriums serving as filters for recycling the air.

Complexes like the Forum Civic Centre in Norwich (1996–2001), the Manchester City Art Gallery (1994–2002) and the Evelina Children's Hospital (1999–2005), and the Wellcome Trust Building (1999–2004) in London are excellent examples of the fluent dialogue between architecture and the city. Freer, sinuous forms demonstrate how research into the thermal properties of materials has led to increasingly advanced results, clear evidence of the importance of research into the potential of all materials, especially traditional ones. This is an interest that diverges from current architectural practice, which sees in the use of glass, because it is purely industrial product, its highest form of expression.

Hopkins's sustainable strategies do not, however, only take on the vagaries of the British climate, but they are also intended to tackle the climatic conditions in such different parts of the world as the Mediterranean, the United Arab Emirates, and Arizona. The organization of the elevations of the GEK-Terna headquarters (2000–03) in Athens is designed to solve the problem of solar gain in the summer months. The buildings in the desert and the project for a business centre in Dubai are practical experiments into how a sustainable approach can be taken even in a country where there is still a lack of awareness regarding the importance of this theme. New techniques for the reduction of thermal bridges are one of the most interesting aspects of building in cities like Dubai, which reaches 45 degrees Celsius with humidity of 90 per cent and where the thermal difference between interiors and exteriors is very marked.

The Joule II research programme funding that has been granted to the practice is confirmation that it is possible to face the future with optimism: Hopkins and the Arup engineers are working on solutions that will allow a better world to be constructed. The partnership between engineering and architecture is of fundamental importance when tackling the issue of sustainability: as Walter Gropius wrote in 1955, "the design of finished buildings, from component parts to their actual assembly on the site, should be solved in a closely integrated collaboration between the architect, the engineer, and the builder, in direct contact with industrial methods and research".

In this spirit Hopkins stated that "our architecture comes out of our engineering and our engineering comes out of our engineers", thus paying homage to the work and research of an integrated team in which architects and engineers participate from the first stages of the project. Thanks to this method, the minimalism of Hopkins's architecture is

Evelina Children's Hospital, London, 1999-2005

The Forum, Norwich, 1996-2001

made even more powerful by a rigorous conception of the structural role, reaffirming the timeless philosophy of Augustus Pugin when he asserted that "all ornament should consist in the essential construction of the building. In pure architecture, the smallest detail should have meaning or purpose". And if, as the Greek architect Aris Konstantinidis stated, 'good architecture starts always with efficient construction', then Hopkins's experimentation of the last few years produces not only good architecture, but also the some of the most interesting buildings in the world today.

[1] R. Banham, *Theory and Design in the First Machine Age*, Architectural Press, London, 1960, p. 135, drawn from the text of the Manifesto of Futurist Architecture, as published in *Rivista Tecnica*, Lugano, 1956, no. 7

[2] R. Banham, *Theory and Design in the First Machine Age*, p. 345

[3] Martin Pawley, *Theory and Design in the Second Machine Age*, Blackwell, London 1990

[4] Colin Davis, *High-Tech Architecture*, Thames and Hudson, London, 1988

[5] John Winter, "Inside Job: Bracken House", *Architects' Journal*, 1992

[6] Walter Gropious, *Scope of Total Architecture*, East Midland Allied Press, 1956

Chapter I

The Foundations of a New Tectonic

Steel and glass technologies were tried out in a group of buildings and a construction system.

The desire to implement the technological transfer from industry to house building led to exploration of the potential of exposed structures and the dematerialization of the construction.

Buckminster Fuller's utopias – associated with his concept of the "ephemeralization" of the project – were wed to boundless faith in progress, in accordance with the best modern tradition. Thus were born the principles of a new tectonic characterizing High Tech in its radical period.

Hopkins House, Hampstead, London, 1975–76
Greene King Brewery Draught Beer Cellars,
Bury St Edmunds, Suffolk, 1977–80
Patera Building System, 1980–82
Hopkins Studio, Marylebone, London 1984
Schlumberger Cambridge Research Centre, 1982–92
Fleet Velmead Infants School, Hampshire, 1984–86
Solid State Logic, Begbroke, Oxon, 1986–88

Hopkins House
Hampstead, London, NW3
1975–76

In 1975 Michael and Patty Hopkins bought a plot of land in Hampstead, in an elegant street lined with Georgian and Regency villas. There, they built their London home, which, thanks to its innovative contribution to steel and glass construction techniques, made its mark in architectural history as one of the icons of modernity.

Hopkins House does not attempt make any concessions to its context; the design concerns were of a different sort, is, as the architects themselves wrote in 1977: "The house was to serve as a home and office for a couple of architects with three children. Our priority was that of making the best use of the surface of the site with a rational and economical steel and glass construction, where the technologies already tried out in the industrial sector could be adopted."

After eight years with Norman Foster, Hopkin's ambition was to transfer to the domestic scale the processes already successfully applied to industrial buildings, in order to demonstrate the full expressive, functional, and performance potential of the new materials and technologies in a housing prototype.

After nearly a generation, the Messianic fascination of Le Corbusier's declaration exhorting "industry to concern itself with the construction and mass-production of the elements of the house" had yet to wane. The "machine for living in" was still part of the utopian vision of Richard Buckminster Fuller, who visited Hopkins House many years after its construction and was deeply impressed.

The aim of the project was the maximum use of the site with the minimum investment of resources, its most evident source of inspiration being the West Coast school, especially the house that Ray and Charles Eames built for themselves at Santa Monica in 1949. However, in 1975, almost thirty years after the Eames's experiment, to build a house by assembling industrial components was no longer a challenge. The Hopkinses' innovation lay in developing a "house-product" characterized by lightness, transparency and, above all, by the maximum economy of materials, techniques and other resources.

The design originates, therefore, from the realization of the most spontaneous solution, almost self-generated from the morphology of the site – but is this not also a form of alternative contextualism?

Thus, a site with an unusually wide frontage, by London standards (14 m), with most of it 3 m below street level, produces a rectangular volume of 12 by 10 m – the longer elevation is reduced by one metre on each side to avoid shared party walls with the adjacent proper-ties – with access from an asymmetrical footbridge leading to the first floor, containing the public area (the office), linked by a central spiral staircase to the ground floor, which is devoted to domestic spaces.

The regular geometry of the plan is reflected by an equally rigorous structural system: a modular grid in light metal elements, a framework of lattice trusses and square steel columns with floors in troughed metal decking. The choice of a small-scale structural unit (4 by 2 m) makes it possible to eliminate the need for a secondary structure: this dematerializes the space and renders it open, transparent, fluid, flexible, and not hierarchical, in line with Buckminster Fuller's contemporary philosophy of the ephemeral.

The two levels (120 sq m each) are flooded with light; eight slender blue columns with Venetian blinds divide the space, creating dynamic views of domestic life. The freestanding pods, containing the bathrooms, which separate the rooms are only concession to privacy. The steel and glass panels forming the light skin of the shell accentuate the fluid permeability of the interior. Profiled metal panels are used for the side walls, sliding glass panels for the front and back: the joints are simple and repetitive and a single frame runs along edges of the floor slabs and the roof.

With today's new environmental awareness, it is interesting to examine the impact of a building without thermal mass. In effect, the heating and cooling of this pioneering glass house is largely natural: during the winter, the south-facing glass façade ensures adequate passive heating and, during the summer, 50 per cent of the glazing can be opened to cool the interior at no energy cost.

Despite the classicism of its minimalist design, Hopkins House is a fine expression of the avant-garde thought of the day, which favoured egalitarian living spaces within the context of non-monumental architecture. Inspired more by Miesian rigour than American experimentalism, Hopkins House does not offer an orthodox concept of family life, even though the pale pearl grey of the fitted carpets, the bright blue of the structure, the vivid red of the Eames's chairs furnishing the interior and the intense green of the vegetation in the garden transform this experimental domestic environment into a work of great vitality and faith in the future. This building was not, however, merely intended to cater for the routine of everyday life, but also to create the ideal setting for communication with prospective clients, who soon started to arrive.

Entrance level

1 footbridge
2 entrance
3 studio
4 shower room
5 bed
6 dressing
7 sitting

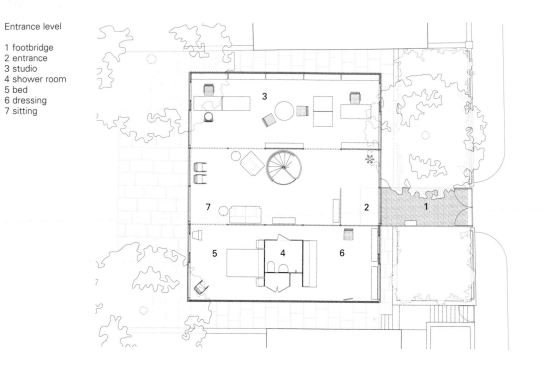

2m

Garden level

1 sitting
2 dining
3 kitchen
4 bedroom
5 shower room
6 garden

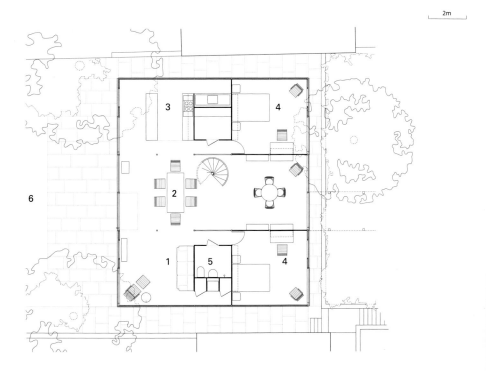

The minimal corner detail

Glazed wall detail

Bottom
The living area
at garden level

500mm

Opposite page
The garden façade

Greene King Brewery Draught Beer Cellars
Bury St Edmunds, Suffolk
1977–80

At the beginning of the 1970s, when Greene King, a well-known British brewer of draught beer, became a player in the mass market, their product required large-scale distribution. Because the old brewery had shortcomings with respect to the distribution of its spaces and its accessibility, the firm decided to construct a new building to house the final stages of the production cycle: washing the casks on arrival; filling them; storing and loading them ready for distribution.

Hopkins solved this complex problem with a simple linear space: a glazed container allowing its contents – and the beating heart that powers this building-machine – to be seen. This architecture comes to life; it lights up, and identifies itself with what is taking place within: architecture without barriers, it is elegantly industrial, the expression and representation of the best machine aesthetic.

One of Hopkins's first experiments with the expressive potential of steel and glass, the Greene King building marks the beginning of a new tectonics that, from a language, became a design discipline, a methodology from which the subsequent work developed.

The building has a compact rectangular form both on plan and in section. The floor is raised one metre off the ground to avoid the danger of flooding from the nearby River Linnett: in any case, this height has the advantage of coinciding with that of the platforms of the vehicles being loaded and unloaded.

The primary structure consists of three rows of tubular columns supporting lattice trusses with tubular struts; on this rests a flat roof in metal sheeting which, on the main elevations, is cantilevered to form a canopy over the loading bay. Along the sides, the transversal beams project from the columns a sufficient distance to allow the creation of full-length perimetrical corridors leading to the emergency exits on the external platform, linked to ground level by two flights of stairs at the corners.

The interior is a flexible container: it is a global space with an open plan, interrupted only by the freestanding "buildings within buildings" that house the ancillary functions – such as the offices, plant, workshops and toilets – and a larger area containing the cool store; the remaining space holds the beer tanks and the machines for washing and filling the casks.

The side elevations, infilled with profiled metal sheeting coated with silver fluorocarbon resin, consist of modules of panels that are perforated only by the two central doors. The front and rear elevations are enhanced by the series of freestanding columns determining the modular arrangement of the two glazed façades.

Apart from the need to solve the problem of flooding, the raising of the building creates an effect of suspension, almost as if it were touching down on arrival from some fantastic location, giving free rein to our imagination in a world where technology is a means for renewing the course of time.

Thus the building is radical High-Tech following the logic of the avant-garde of the period, Minimalist in its aesthetic, and refinedly Rationalist in the way it integrates form and function, the container and its contents. The main glazed elevation, raised from the ground and crowned by the deep cantilever inevitably recalls a stage: a theatre transcending the functionalism of the factory where, in the evening, the lights go on and it becomes the spectacle in itself.

Cutaway axonometric view

1 unloading yard
2 washing and racking
3 beer tanks
4 plant
5 cooled full store
6 pantry
7 loading yard

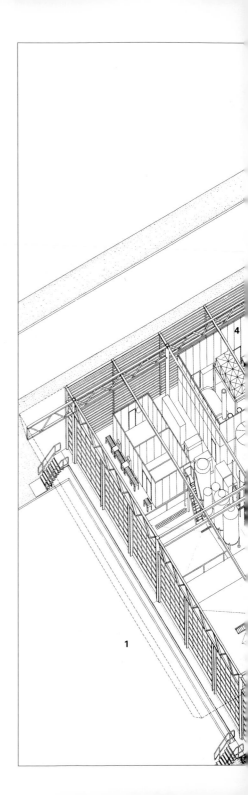

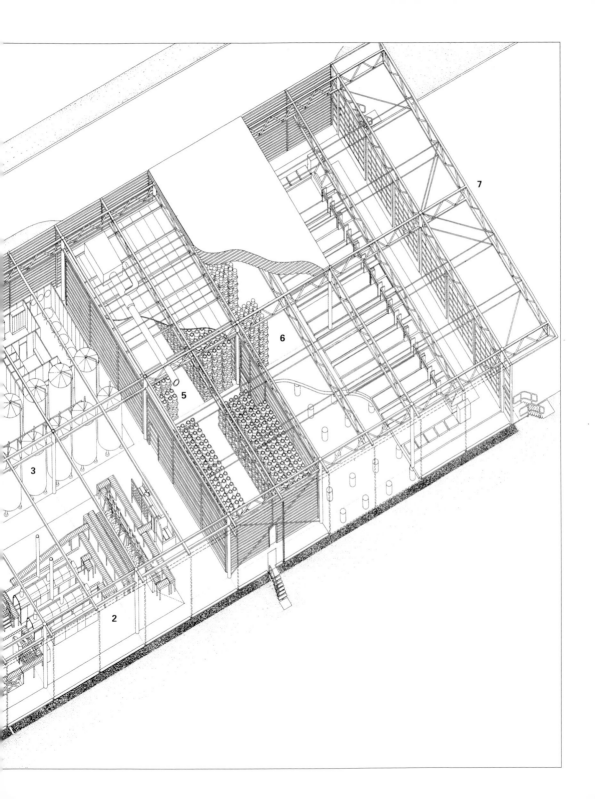

Day and night views
of the building

Opposite page
The building is elevated
above the floor plain to the
loading height of a brewery
dray lorry

Patera Building System
1980–82

In 1920 Le Corbusier wrote: "From the point of view of architecture, I put myself in the state of mind of the inventor of the aeroplane." It was in this spirit that Hopkins devised the Patera building system, which, the client, Nigel Dale, believed would meet the industrial market's demand for medium-sized prefabricated buildings.

This was an ideal commission for Hopkins, who had long been interested in architecture seen as a product, the architecture-machine to be realized with industrial processes, to be transported and assembled as a kit, with the most efficient use of materials and other resources.

To paraphrase Le Corbusier, Patera is "a machine for work that utilizes standardization to address the problem of perfection": it is a "skin and bones" container with 216 sq m of floor area and 3.5 m of height that can be assembled just about anywhere in no more than 10 days.

Thanks to the refined design of the components, the steel- and glass-clad steel structure creates an iconic space, the expression of the radical new spirit that the fathers of the Modern Movement had aspired to, but which was not actually engendered until the High-Tech architects brought to their own sphere technological know-how from fields extraneous to building, such as the aerospace industry.

The structural framework consists of a portal composed of tubular lattice trusses external to the building. The decision to expose the structure produced immediate advantages, such as avoiding the constraints of the fire regulations, which do not apply to external structural work, and allowing a notable saving of material and related construction and maintenance costs, but, above all, it endowed the architecture with an exclusive, easily recognizable identity. There are, on the other hand, disadvantages of a structural nature: an external frame is subject to rapid deterioration, also due to the strain resulting from the dynamic loads.

The Patera system technology solves this problem by means of an ingenious engineering device: the portal is a rigid frame only in appearance, because a restraining boom with a special hinged rod in the centre of the span makes it, in effect, a hybrid structure; it functions as a three-pin structure under permanent loads and as a two-pin structure when it reacts to the force of the wind.

The elegance of the design is enhanced by the continuity of the cladding material, stressing the pure geometry of the volume. The infilling consists of sandwich panels made with mineral fibre insulation between two sheets of ribbed pressed steel supported by a secondary structure of rectangular hollow-section purlins. The wiring and water pipes run through ducts within the thickness of the panels.

Axonometric showing
construction sequence

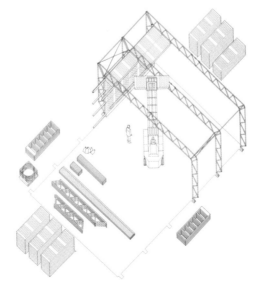

A whole Patera building can
be erected by forklift truck

Following pages
One of two Patera units
constructed at Canary
Wharf, London,1985

Hopkins Studio
Marylebone, London, NW1
1984

Only six Patera buildings have been built, two in Marylebone where they house the Hopkins office; one of the two varies slightly from the first prototype. Building One fronting the street, built in 1984, was in fact, a more advanced version of the building system: the height has been increased in order to house a mezzanine floor; glass panels have also been inserted in the roof and the framework has been replaced with a more classical structure of trusses on tubular-steel columns.

In 1995 the campus was extended, Building Two, a version of the original Patera building, and a glazed reception area were constructed. All are now linked by a walkway covered with a tensile fabric structure.

It is significant that the architect has chosen to locate his office in these buildings, which, besides marking the beginning of Hopkins's exploration of steel and glass construction systems form a cultural link with the Modern Movement and herald its radical epilogue.

An early view of the office

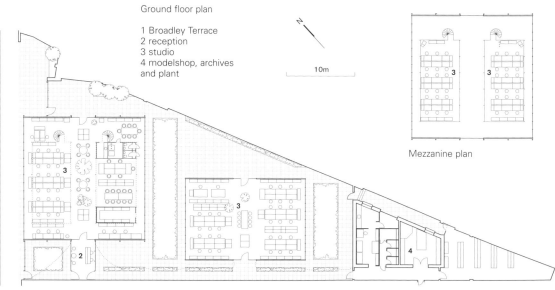

Ground floor plan

1 Broadley Terrace
2 reception
3 studio
4 modelshop, archives and plant

10m

Mezzanine plan

Schlumberger Cambridge Research Centre
Cambridgeshire
1982–92

Following pages
The winter garden, which
forms a restaurant and
social space for
Schlumberger staff

Phase 1 (1982–85)

The Schlumberger Cambridge Research Centre is one of the two main research facilities of a French multinational providing technical support to companies in the oil industry. Founded in 1927 by the brothers Conrad and Marcel Schlumberger, it is an international group that projects its corporate image also through architecture (its Connecticut administration building is by Phillip Johnson and Howard Barnstone, the rehabilitation of the Schlumberger industrial site in Paris is by Renzo Piano).

In 1982 Michael Hopkins received the commission for the project for the new centre in Cambridge, which is concerned with drilling, fluid mechanics, physics of rocks and agglomerates, and computerized three-dimensional modelling of the data obtained by the drilling.

The site covers seven hectares, and can be accessed from the M11 motorway, just a few minutes from the centre of Cambridge, also by way of a bike-and footpath. There are two buildings, which were constructed in two separate phases: the first (5,600 sq m) houses a simulated drilling rig, offices, laboratories, a conference room and the staff restaurant; the second (6,400 sq m) has further spaces for offices and laboratories.

The client's requirements were clear and regarded mainly the distributional relationships between the four different uses of the spaces: laboratories, offices, the test hall and the area for socialization. In the traditional building type, the activities with a high level of noise pollution (the noise in the drilling area can reach 85–90 dBA) would be isolated, while the project sought the greatest possible integration among (both the theoretical computer-based studies and the experimental research) Hopkins made courageous choices, proposing a design where all the functions coexisted in a single organism, a solution in a single space with clearly defined limits that generated a single compact volume. This methodology has continued to inform the architect's approach to design until the present day.

These preliminaries resulted in a simple and clear plan: a central space covered with three bays of a spectacular Teflon coated glass fibre membrane roof and flanked by two wings. The central space contains two separate areas: to the north, the area for experimentation with oilfield equipment where there are three shafts 20 m in depth for testing drilling techniques and a high-pressure underground pump; to the south, a winter garden housing the reception and relaxation areas (including a library and a restaurant). The side wings, housing the service facilities (laboratories and offices), have sound insulation provided by laminated glass (21 mm), and are infilled clad with full-height sliding glass panels that stress the continuity of the series of volumes.

The principles underlying the plan are inspired by Louis Kahn's distinction between "served" and "serving" spaces: the offices for the scientists are located along the perimeter of the building and are separated by a circulation route from the laboratories giving onto the large central space. Each block of the two wings is divided into five modules separated by the entrances; a recess in the façade creates a small entrance porch for each one. This modular division recalls the Patera system, although there is a difference in the details: for instance, tubular-steel columns, not vertical lattice trusses, support the external lattice roof trusses, although this also stemmed from the need to accelerate the construction of the building. The structural system is independent from that of the side blocks and functions as the load-bearing structure of the Teflon-coated glass-fibre roof that allows 13 per cent of the daylight to filter through, giving a quasi-external feeling to the space.

Entirely constructed in steel with metal or glass facing, the building is crowned by a system of cables and masts supporting the radical High-Tech tent-like roof used for the first time on a large scale in this project, and subsequently becoming the architect's trademark.

The air-conditioning plant is housed in the plant rooms in the basement, the electrical services in the ducts under the raised floors.

The Schlumberger Centre is the result of research and innovation: it is an architectural prototype that has its conceptual roots in the exploratory work undertaken by Eero Saarinen and Mies van der Rohe, which Hopkins continues with new constructional and environmental developments, such as the use of glazed systems on a large scale, the structural use of glass fibre, the air treatment of large internal spaces, the functional integration and the flexibility of the spaces.

Despite its essentially industrial purpose, the complex adorns the rural landscape on the outskirts of Cambridge thanks to its architecture formed of lightness and transparency that adds poetic value to the dichotomy between artifice and nature.

Phase 2 (1990–92)

The flexible modular design of the first building would have permitted the addition of further units to the linear plan of the wings, which were intended to be adapted to future developments, but the new directions of research, now with a more theoretical slant, no longer required direct contact between the laboratories and the test drilling area. This brought greater freedom to the design of the extension, giving rise to a new block, thereby transforming the centre into what is effectively a research campus.

The plans required new spaces for offices, laboratories, computer and conference rooms, and a reception area that were all to be housed in an independent building situated at one end of the first building along the north-south axis. This new block comprises two symmetrical wings linked by a glazed central atrium forming the new entrance, where the reception area for the whole complex is located. Its permeability and transparency help to integrate the new building with the pre-existing one, and together they provide a dynamic sequence of views. Following a procedure based on the updating of techniques already acquired – but never stereotyped – this new project develops systems previously applied to the Solid State Logic building (at Begbroke, near Oxford): the wings have a square plan and are two storeys in height: the first floor overhangs the ground level; all-glass walls are screened by Venetian blinds and the floors consist of reinforced concrete slabs supported by cylindrical steel columns. The plan has the same distributive layout as the Solid State Logic building, except for the fact that the double height of the central space has been replaced here with laboratories, plant rooms, a computer suite and a conference rooms, a natural choice at the baricentre of activities.

This continuity in the underlying design is enriched by numerous innovative elements in the design of both the structure and the plant.

The reinforced concrete floors were not cast *in situ*, but were made with prefabricated elements: this was the first step towards the larger-scale use of prefabrication in future projects. A shallow coffered formwork, made from sand and cement sprayed onto a welded steel mesh, was completed with a topping of concrete: the curved profiles of the formwork conform approximately to the stresses of the structure, creating a pattern on the exposed soffit that recalls the ribbing along the isostatic lines adopted by Pier Luigi Nervi in 1954 for the Gatti Wool Factory, near Rome.

The illumination and air grilles are not part of a later phase of operations, but are cast into the concrete floorslabs with horizontal services located under the raised floor above.

The flat roof also represents a step forward from the one used at Begbroke: the framework of trusses has been replaced by a grillage of steel beams on a square module of 3.6 m, with graphite iron spheroidal cruciform castings.

An important innovation regards the roof of the atrium, which is not supported by the network of cables as in the Begbroke building, but with a pneumatic system. Each structural bay is covered with an inflated cushion formed by three layers of transparent fluorocarbon film: each layer is welded to gaskets fitted to aluminium extrusions and the air pressure is controlled automatically.

In this spatial and technological tour de force, Hopkins demonstrated that, at the beginning of the 1990s, he had already mastered the know-how that would allow him to undertake new explorations of the most complex relationships between building and architecture and the urban environment.

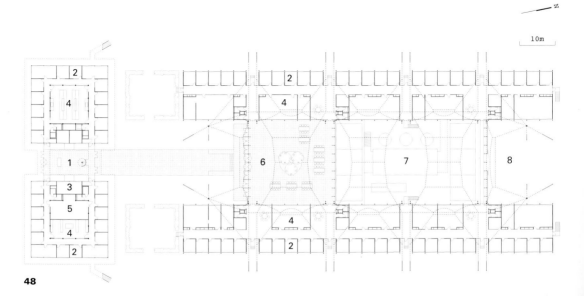

Opposite page
Ground floor plan

1 entrance hall
2 offices
3 meeting room
4 laboratory
5 plant
6 winter garden
7 test station
8 service yard

The Phase 2 entrance

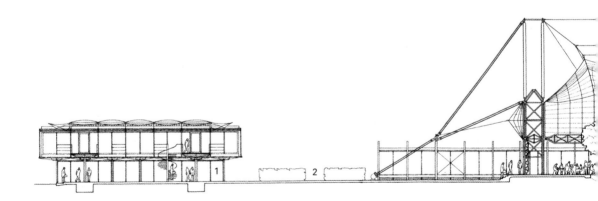

Long section through site

1 entrance hall
2 courtyard
3 winter garden
4 drilling test pits
5 test station
6 service yard

10m

50

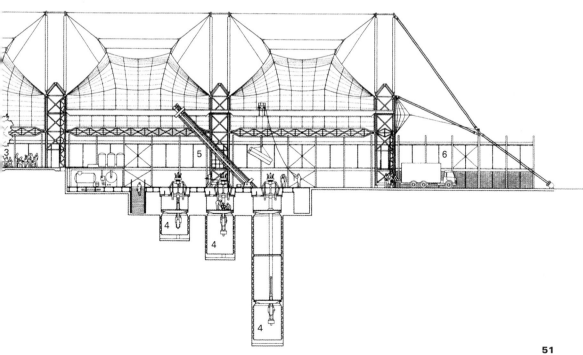

Fleet Velmead Infants School
Hampshire
1984–86

Hampshire County Council is renowned both for encouraging experimentation and for the avant-garde spirit of many of its new buildings. In 1984 Sir Colin Stansfield-Smith commissioned Hopkins to design an innovative school with unconventional spaces intended to stimulate the children's learning process. The new school was to replace an old Victorian building.

Hopkins proposed an open-plan building covered with a glass fibre membrane structure that the practice was testing for a centre in Basildon, in collaboration with engineers from Buro Happold. This project was rejected by the council's education committee on the grounds that it was excessively innovative. Hopkins abandoned the membrane structure, but kept the basic idea of a flexible building with a single roof. The new project comprised a block with a rectangular plan divided longitudinally by a corridor covered with a domed skylight from which the double-pitched aluminium roof slopes down. A spine corridor separates the space into two identical halves, subdivided by free-standing partitions into areas where the various teaching activities take place.

The school is an experiment in constructive poetics expressed by the technological details and the purity of the geometries and surfaces: a fully glazed volume supported by a slender structure of circular steel columns linked to the secondary structure of cables, tie rods and struts by means of flanges and pins. All the components are clearly in evidence in accordance with the elegant logic of the design; only the purlins supporting the roof are partially hidden in the roof decking, leaving just the tubular bottom boom exposed beneath the soffit. This is a device that endows the structure with a sense of suspension, so that it seems to float on the glass panels of the façades.

Rather than the space, it is the proportions, the structural dimensioning, the materials and details that become the priority design considerations.

The original plan's glass fibre structure survives only in part, in the row of coloured awnings shading the south elevation: this is an element that has the function of preventing excessive solar gain as well as adding a note of gaiety and playfulness to the school.

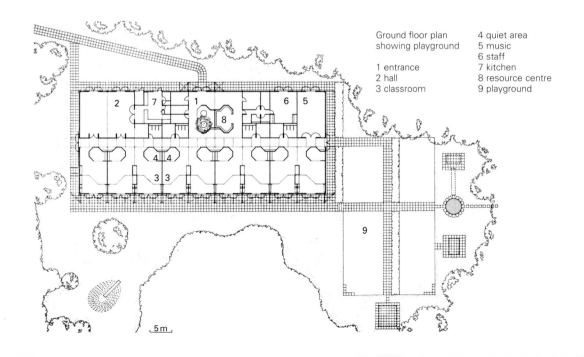

Ground floor plan showing playground

1 entrance
2 hall
3 classroom
4 quiet area
5 music
6 staff
7 kitchen
8 resource centre
9 playground

5 m

The play terrace showing
the canopy shading

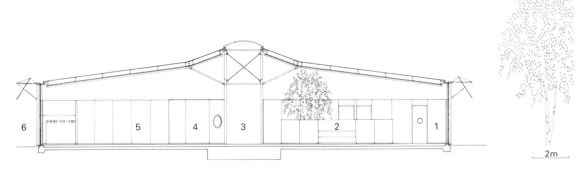

Cross section

1 entrance
2 resource area
3 circulation spine
4 quiet area
5 classroom
6 paved play area

2m

Following pages
The school viewed from
the south

Solid State Logic
Begbroke, Oxon, Oxfordshire
1986–88

Solid State Logic, a manufacturer of sound-recording and broadcasting equipment, occupied various buildings in the Oxfordshire countryside – including an old garage, three industrial sheds and a custom-designed building resembling a church at Stonesfield, near Oxford – when they commissioned Hopkins to design their new headquarters, to house both their offices and production facilities.

Abandoning any typological stereotype, the design maintained a strong industrial look expressed by an innovative layout and the advanced technology of the construction details. The square plan of the building is reflected in various aspects of its design: the flat roof, pierced by a central roof light illuminating the two-storey atrium around which the circulation is arranged, underscores the geometric regularity. The ground floor houses the production area with the laboratories located along the perimeter; on the first floor, the offices and service areas are separated by glass panels to allow maximum flexibility in the arrangement of the spaces. The pure geometry of the plan and elevations is stressed by the clean-cut line of the projecting first-floor slab that emphasizes the juxtaposition of the two glazed volumes: this is a classic strategy that, in this case, creates an unprecedented sense of suspension of the box-like form. The effect is further accentuated by the depth of the shadow in the portico, which, in addition to exalting the apparent challenge to the laws of statics, protects the ground floor from excessive solar gain in the summer months.

The structure is made up of circular steel columns and reinforced concrete floor slabs: on the ground floor the grid is based on a module of 7.2 m, which is doubled on the first floor.

The language of material expressed through their assembly techniques comunicates the strength of a design that unify architectural and structural hierarchy: each element - from the column, to the elegant suspended ceiling in panels of perforated aluminium, the glass envelope, the concrete slab of the portico – has a clear aesthetic and constructional role that determines a harmonic (balanced) whole through the sum of its individual parts.

Despite the fact that its is almost entirely glazed, with the exception of the louvres of the plant rooms, the building conveys a sense of solidity and permanence thanks to the compactness of its volumes and the textures of the different components, such as the concrete first floor slab with shallow domed coffers cast in it to take light fittings and a shot-blasted finish.

The building services are located under the raised floor and in the suspended ceiling under the roof.

Together with the intensive use of glass, the project includes sustainable devices, such as the building's compact layout, which is intended to minimize heat loss; and the glass panels that can be shaded with external Venetian blinds and opened to full height to allow natural ventilation, as well as being tinted grey. The building is surrounded by a garden with mature trees, visible and accessible not only from the ground floor but also from the first floor by the four staircases at the corners.

In short, this is a very refined building that avoids any excess of technicality thanks to a Miesian rigour, combined with the constructive honesty typical of British architecture.

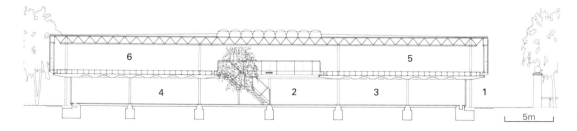

5m

Section through atrium

1 entrance
2 atrium

3 console assembly
4 component assembly
5 administration
6 research and development

Opposite page
Solid State Logic is a
transparent and open
building set in a woodland
garden

First floor plan

1 administration
2 atrium
3 research and
development

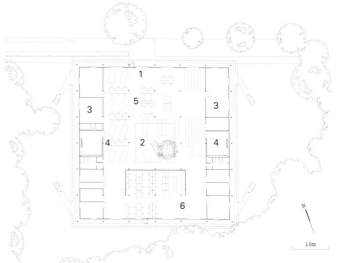

Ground floor plan

1 entrance
2 atrium
3 test rooms
4 plant
5 console assembly
6 component assembly

Chapter 2

Technology and Context:
Towards a Theory of Architecture

The years spent reflecting on the significance of innovation have opened up new horizons. Architecture as a product encounters urban complexity. Buckminster Fuller's utopias are combined with the ethics of Ruskin and Pugin: the tools offered by emerging technologies formulate a grammar that transforms the narrative of building into new expressive results.

Reconciliation with history begins with a process of synthesis in which tradition is no longer a myth but rather dynamic continuity.

Mound Stand, Lord's Cricket Ground, London, 1984–87
Bracken House, London, 1987–92
David Mellor Cutlery Factory, Hathersage, Sheffield, 1988–89
David Mellor Offices and Showroom, London, 1988–91
Tottenham Court Road Station, London, 1990–
New Square, New Square, Bedfont Lakes, London, 1989–92
Glyndebourne Opera House, Sussex, 1989–94

Mound Stand
Lord's Cricket Ground
London, NW8
1984–87

The Mound Stand is Hopkins's first work in an historical urban context: innovation and continuity both characterize the project, which is based on an ingenious system of static equilibria that, with an elegant synthesis, give an account – through the progressive dematerialization of the elevation on St John's Wood Road – of the development of technology from the nineteenth century to modern times. Lord's Cricket Ground is located in a conservation area of Marylebone, where one is inevitably aware of tradition represented by the older buildings and by a sport, cricket, that is the very symbol of Englishness. It is no coincidence that Hopkins refers to this project as his "reconciliation with history". On the occasion of its bicentenary in 1984, the Marylebone Cricket Club held a competition for the reconstruction of the stand designed in the 1890s by Frank Verity: all that was to remain of the old stand were the tiers of seats and part of the base, consisting of a six-arch brick arcade terminating in a by-then badly deteriorated metal structure. Hopkins's project won because it guaranteed speed of execution with minimum disturbance to the cricket season, thanks to the rebuilding and extension of the brick arcade and the use of prefabricated components for the new stand.

The result is a cohesive structure in layers, where different materials and techniques recount the history of technology from the Victorian age to the present day: from brickwork to fabric membrane structures, from solidity to dematerialization. In a progression towards the immaterial, the project starts with a massive contact with the ground and proceeds with a continuous lightening of the material: brick is followed by glass blocks, steel, glass and finally the soaring fabric tent roofs attached to masts pointing towards the ultimate transparency, the sky. The main elevation, on St John's Wood Road, is a clearly decipherable composition combining different materials and techniques into a single structure, the leitmotif of which is the Ruskinian candour of its subsystems: an arcade with twenty-seven solid-brick arches, glass-block infill panels, a box (2.6 m in height) made of profiled steel sheeting, reinforced glass panelling and a polyester fibre tensile structure.

The six renovated arches of the pre-existing arcade were extended with twenty-one solid brick arches, which completed the work of Verity, with whom, a century later, Hopkins discovered that he shared the same passion and the same building philosophy. The principles that Gothic Revivalist Augustus Pugin taught Verity met with the approval of Hopkins, who undertook the restoration of the Victorian fragment not as an operation of archaeological interest, but with the aim of integrating the old with the new, thus demonstrating that he identified himself with an old school of thought that he still finds relevant today. The extension of the unfinished arcade solved the problem of the building's contact with the ground and its relationship with the pre-existing structure and the urban context, while the use of modern materials and technologies in the new stand created an innovative construction in dynamic equilibrium with the brick base.

The structure is curved in order to maintain the Mound's excellent view of the ground as well as to generate feelings of camaraderie between spectators, stimulating their participation in the sporting event. A key feature of the project is the innovative structural system consisting of six slender circular steel columns secured to a steel plate girder running the full length of the building; trusses (equivalent to the span of an arch) are attached to this at regular intervals with flanges and bolts. To this primary structural framework of columns, girder and trusses are attached the beams supporting the floor of the second level of tiers.

The six steel columns of the primary structure are placed eccentrically to the load, which, obviously, is greater on the side nearer the ground: this stratagem is of fundamental importance for the creation of the static system that subjects the main elevation, on St John's Wood Road, to traction. The structure is completed by the fabric membrane roof attached to masts and cables, which are connected to the steel columns of the primary structure and discharge their load to the ground along tie rods fixed to the brick base. This innovative system leaves a clear view of the ground and – using a creative and not merely opportunistic device – resolves the whole project. The final effect is that of an exercise in static equilibrium, emphasized by suspension of the tiers of seats and the dynamic tension of the fabric roof, which, besides being the architect's trademark, pays homage to the origins of cricket, a summer sport that has always been associated with marquees on village greens.

The tensile structure consists of eleven polyester fabric cones: six, centred on the steel columns and having a diameter equivalent to two brick arches, and five higher ones, having a diameter equivalent to three arches. Once again, there is a geometric pattern producing an unusual roofline that helps to complete a project where every single element is conceived with rational creativity and elegant aesthetic and structural minimalism.

Section through Mounds
Stand

1 lower terrace seating
2 upper terrace seating
3 arcade
4 bars and wcs
5 private boxes
6 private dining rooms
7 corridor
8 mezzanine level
9 debenture seats
10 restaurant

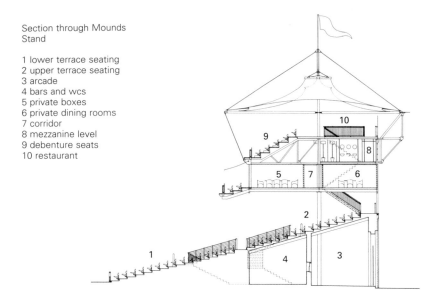

Upper promenade level

Lower promenade level

Terrace level

Arcade level

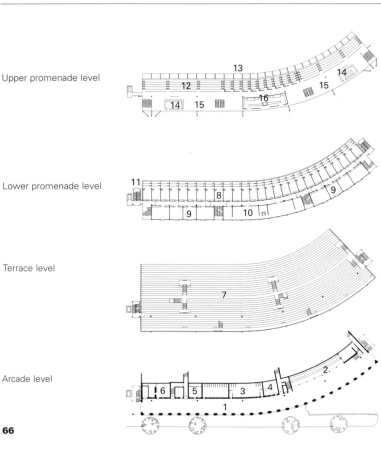

1 arcade
2 arcade bar
3 public wcs
4 shop
5 chief steward
6 police
7 terrace seating
8 private boxes
9 private dining room
10 kitchens
11 lift
12 debenture seating
13 private viewing boxes
14 upper-level bar
15 restaurant
16 servery

Sheltered from rain and sun
beneath the fabric roof

The layered façade

Opposite page
The spectators' viewpoint

Bracken House
London, EC4
1987–92

In 1952 Brendan Bracken, the chairman of the *Financial Times*, commissioned Sir Albert Richardson to design Bracken House, a new building for the newspaper on a site near St Paul's Cathedral. Richardson was inspired by the Italian Baroque palaces, especially the Palazzo Carignano in Turin, built by Guarino Guarini in 1697. He took Guarini's characteristic elliptical volume and simplified it, creating a central building with an octagonal plan to house the printing works, flanked by two seven-floor wings where the administrative and editorial offices were located.

The client expressly requested that the building be salmon pink in colour, like the paper on which the newspaper is printed: thus pink Hollington stone was used for the base and pink-red bricks were specially made for the wings.

Around the middle of the 1980s the *Financial Times* moved its editorial offices to Southwark and started construction of the new print works in the Docklands, now becoming a major development area to the east of the City. In 1987 Bracken House was the first postwar building to be included on the list of protected buildings. A Japanese construction company, the Obayashi Corporation, subsequently acquired it, and decided to transform it into offices that were to be leased to the Industrial Bank of Japan. They commissioned Hopkins to adapt the building to the needs of modern offices, while still respecting the setting and the prestigious pre-existing building.

The new project maintained the side blocks but demolished the central building to make way for a radial-plan volume with, in the centre, a rectangular atrium: this form was the result of superimposing Palazzo Carignano's two central ellipses onto the Bracken House plan. The new elliptical volume comprises a large central space and offices along its perimeter: this layout reinforces the functional link with the two wings, whereas, previously, the printing works had always formed a barrier. Moreover, the gentle curves of the plan are able to accommodate the different angles and lines of the retained wings without altering the overall arrangement. Richardson's late classicism is reinterpreted in the division of the façade, which consists of three horizontal bands: the base, the *piano nobile* (albeit of four floors) and the attic.

The wings were given a new function for small offices, toilets and escape staircases and service risers that that allowed the central building to be kept completely open: the purity and flexibility of the latter space is stressed by the presence, in the centre, of a glass tower for the lifts.

The structure is a classic framework of reinforced concrete beams and columns: radial beams terminate on a ring of columns set back from the building's perimeter. The façade is an exercise in sophisticated technology: from the stone columns of the base project bronze brackets, reinforced from behind by steel rods, onto which the grids of columns supporting the four floors of full-height bay windows discharge their load: these bronze columns are attached to the beams along the edges of the floors, forming string-courses across the façade. An original equilibrium of the forces allows the façade to form a load-bearing construction dividing the elevation between large glazed surfaces and the elegant bronze structural grid with its modular rhythm, interrupted by the constructive virtuosity of the glass canopy projecting over the entrance.

Guarini's classical grammar has been updated with innovative techniques that find precedents in works of the past, such as Oriel Chambers in Liverpool, built by Peter Ellis in 1865. In Bracken House, the materials function according to Gothic-inspired principles of construction that establish dialogue with the pre-existing buildings, thus consolidating a method that transforms the narrative of the construction into new architectural forms.

The original Bracken House
building

Guarino Guarini, Palazzo
Carignano, Turin, 1679

Early sketches showing
the proposal

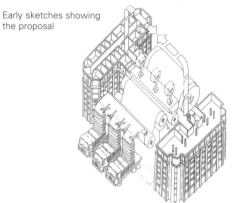

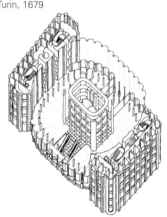

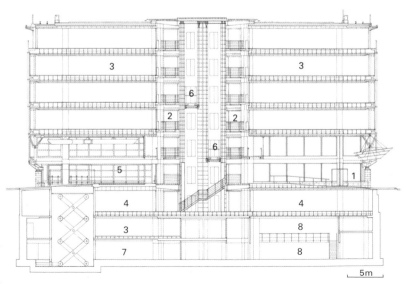

Section through
atrium and lift shalft

1 main entrance
2 atrium
3 new office area
4 dealer floor
5 loading bay
6 lift
7 car park
8 service area

5m

Opposite page
View of the internal atrium

Exploded isometric view
of bay components

1 gunmetal column
2 column connector
3 precast concrete beam
4 steel permanent formwork
5 cast gunmetal base
bracket
6 fairlaced concrete bay slab
7 stainless steel rocker
bearing
8 stainless steel tension rod
9 in-situ concrete column
10 loasbearing Hollington
stone pier
11 perforated steel ceiling
planks
12 light-sensitive blind
control
13 perimeter light fittings
14 venetian blinds
15 toughened double-glazed
suspended bay window
16 bronze smoke vents
17 fan cowl unit
18 pressed bronze coiling
19 raised computer floor

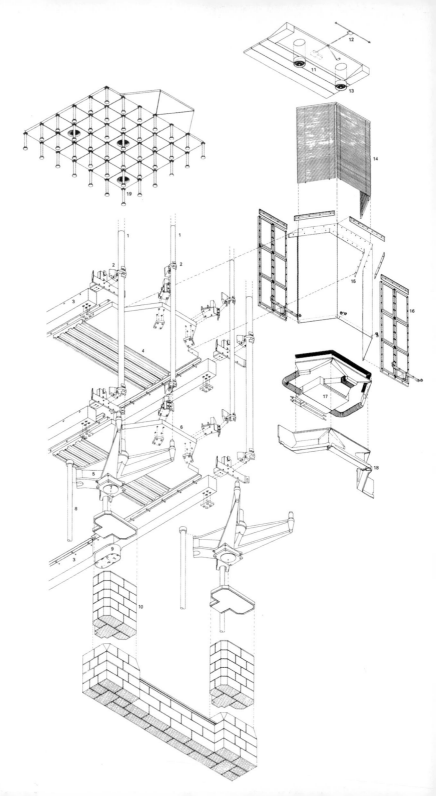

74

The final composition

David Mellor Cutlery Factory
Hathersage, Sheffield
1988–89

David Mellor's renowned firm producing cutlery, kitchenware and tableware is, in Britain, a byword for quality, thanks to the craftsman-like attention to the manufacturing process, directly controlled from design to finished product. A native of Sheffield, city of steel, Mellor opened a workshop and design studio there in the early 1950s, launching his professional career: today one of his sets of silver cutlery is in the Victoria and Albert Museum.

It is clear, therefore, that the decision to move the firm from Sheffield to the nearby village of Hathersage represented an opportunity for Mellor to be directly involved in the design and construction process: he produced some components himself, applying his industrial production know-how to the building sector. The result is a building designed and constructed with special attention to the details, where design and prefabrication are wedded through the assembly of one-off pieces made with great precision and quality.

In 1985 British Gas decided to close an old gasworks in the Peak District National Park in Derbyshire, consisting of a number of stone buildings and two gasholders. David Mellor acquired the complex and commissioned Hopkins to design the new factory, which, as had to follow the local authority planning guidelines, and fit in with the surroundings and reflect the local vernacular.

The circular plan of the new building derives from the foundations (26 m in diameter) of one of the old gasholders: this choice allowed an immediate saving of resources and integrated the new construction into the landscape as naturally as possible. The base of the new building is a concrete slab that projects 90 cm from the previous perimeter, on which stands a round construction, built of local stone and with four openings.

Another constraint – the need to have an open space free from columns – was, once again, turned to advantage in the design with a self-supporting roof that seems almost to float above the circular wall. This is a rigid structure consisting of twenty-four radial steel trusses spanning from padstones in the wall to a conical ring truss: on this structure rests the roof decking of Finnish plywood sandwich panels covered with lead sheeting, with cylindrical joints aligned with those of the wood panels below.

The gently sloping roof made with traditional materials is, in effect, an innovative system of functionally collaborating layers, which include a ventilation system to reduce condensation on the lead. The roof is crowned with a glass lantern, ingeniously supported by an internal structure of radial tie rods forming a bicycle-wheel-like structure linked to the conical ring truss supporting the main radial trusses.

A circular strip window separates the roof from the wall, so that appears to be floating above it without any direct contact, and this creates fascinating light effects inside the building.

The technological structure of the roof embellishes the architectural minimalism: its circular form is reiterated by the massive wall built of local stone with finishings and fair-faced concrete quoins indicating the entrances.

As in Hopkins's previous projects, the geometrical purity is exalted, but not compromised, by interaction with secondary elements: in this case, the roof does not have a gutter so as to avoid interfering with the clarity of the form; rainwater is collected at ground level by a channel surrounding the building. Inside, the space is open and unhindered; the plant and noisy machinery are contained in two free-standing rectangular boxes.

Despite its traditional appearance, this is a building that is extremely innovative in concept, using construction methods where technology is borrowed from industrial production to modernise the materials and techniques of the local vernacular.

This dichotomy between the local vernacular (expressed by the use of stone walls) and innovative technological elements (such as the sophisticated construction of the roof) was to become an open and continuous dialogue in the architecture of Hopkins, who, in this period, was developing the experimental approach that was to characterize many of his more complex future projects. In them there is the proto-rationalist spirit typical of the best Victorian industrial buildings updated by the sophisticated use of modern engineering.

The round building

Roof plan

1 radial steel truss
2 circular steel purlins
3 cross bracing
4 conical ring truss
5 central glazed rooflight
6 lead-clad plywood

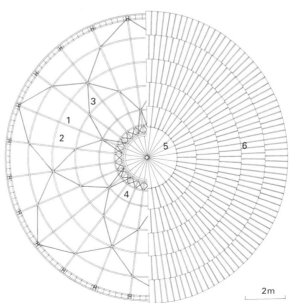

2m

Opposite page and right
Views of the roof structure.

Detail section through
roof and wall

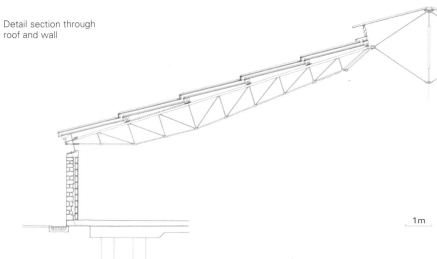

1m

David Mellor Offices and Showroom
Shad Thames, London, SE1
1988–91

This second building for David Mellor houses the designer's showroom and offices, as well as a penthouse flat. As with the factory at Hathersage, the context is linked to the industrial culture of the nineteenth century, even though Shad Thames, a street in Bermondsey, just to the south of Tower Bridge, has a strong urban character. On this occasion, too, Mellor was not only the client, but he was also closely involved in the design process and in the supervision of the construction.

The building consists of a simple glazed block six storeys in height, crowned by the projection of the continuous balconies and the balustrade of the rooftop terrace. The columns and the floor slabs divide up the elevations of the building, which is flanked by two towers set back from the façade: one contains the stairs and lift; the other, the services and technical rooms. The clear separation between the "served" and "servant" spaces has further emphasized the minimalism of these spaces and the construction components, which express their role with great rigour, honesty and clarity of detail.

The narrowness of the building allows the interior to be ventilated naturally, without need for complex air-conditioning plants, which would have required raised floors and suspended ceilings, thus altering the proportions of the design.

The structure, a framework of beams and round columns in fair-faced concrete, did not require special treatment for the fire regulations and has thus been able to maintain all the expressive power of its materials which is what characterizes the style of the project and gives the design its identity.

The main elevation is divided up by the structural grid and the modular frame of the full-height sliding windows inserted between the columns, with a similar use of detail on both the exterior and interior faces: this is technological virtuosity expresses maximum adherence to the logic of honesty of construction, linked to the naturally expressive language of the techniques of the materials. The side elevations are infilled with steel-framed panels covered with lead.

The aim is to exploit the resources in order to release the full expressive potential of the materials, a form of structural minimalism that is certainly not easily achieved. Hopkins and Mellor have spared no effort in perfecting the appropriate execution techniques, from the choice of the type and size of the formwork – which guarantees precision and, at the same time, maintains the desired finish for the concrete – to the design of the joints, of which there are two types: recessed, with aluminium extrusions; projecting, with elegantly chamfered corners.

In-situ execution was, therefore, planned from the very beginning of the preliminary design and careful control of the whole construction process, guaranteed the quality of the final result.

The two towers are clad with flanged steel panels bolted together, like in shipbuilding, with virtually no separation between structure and cladding. The result is an innovative and refined design, made possible by the fact that there was no need for heating, insulation or lining.

According to the founding philosophy of High-Tech, a building is the result of the sum of legible elements that have the dual role of structure and expression. The central block and the two towers are the main volumes on which are inserted the various sub-components, such as the framework, cladding, fixtures, railings and platforms of the balconies, finished so they remain clearly identifiable as separate elements.

Although this project is faithful to the Structuralist philosophy – in contrast to the radical kit of parts, to be assembled just as it comes – it moves closer to the New Brutalist style with the expressivity of its materials: this would lead to Hopkins's future investigation of the uses of traditional materials in a contemporary context.

Exploded isometric view

1 car park
2 showroom
3 offices
4 apartment
5 services
6 stair and lift tower

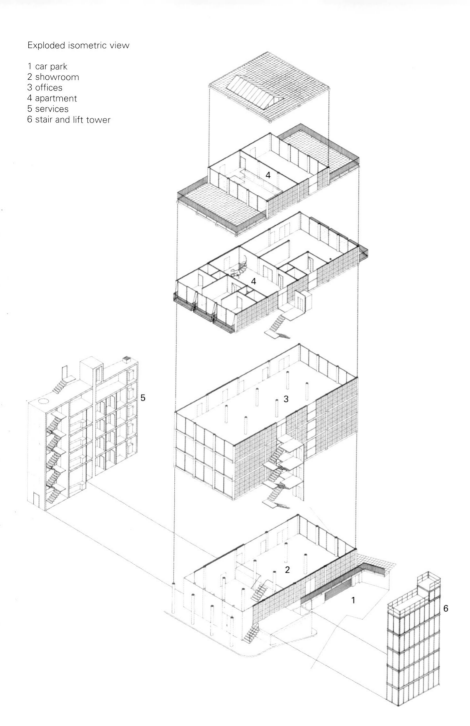

The shop window

Entrance to offices
and penthouse

Tottenham Court Road Station
Westminster, London, WC1
1990–
project

The project for the new Tottenham Court Road underground station envisages the demolition of the existing buildings and the creation of a new corner block consisting of a steel and glass building with four cylindrical towers at its corners.

The key element of the plan is the diagonal pedestrian route through the middle of the building, which continues the colonnade of the external perimeter where the shops are located. The main station ticket hall occupies an oval space below the large atrium at street level, around which are located five floors of offices.

This was one of Hopkins's first urban projects offering a foretaste of elements that the architect was later to develop: the choice of the single block and the clear geometric legibility of the plan, which was equally evident in the composition of the elevations.

Below and opposite page
A model of the building and
its underground network

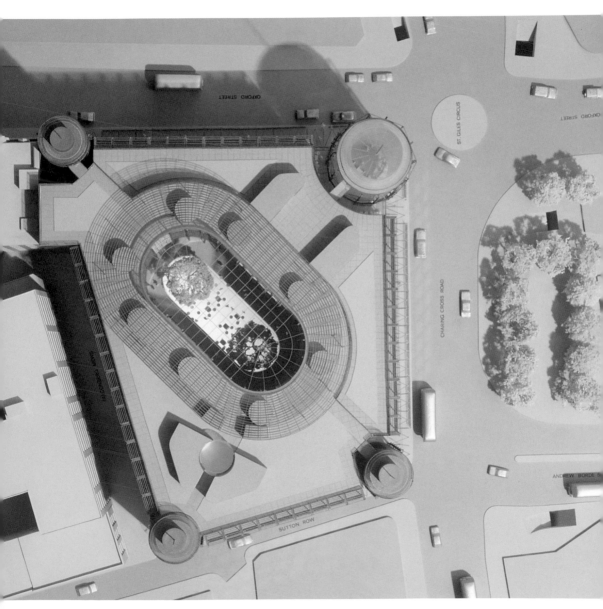

New Square
Bedfont Lakes, London, TW14
1989–92

The master plan for the Bedfont Lakes' business park was an opportunity for an in-depth study of the urban dimension of the project. A new awareness of the relationship between building and context came together, opening a new line of investigation for the potential of technology and the significance of space-time in architecture.

An agreement with the local authority eased approval of the plan: a large area of wasteland would be made into a country park in exchange for planning permission for offices suitable for multinational companies close to London's Heathrow Airport.

A similar kind of development had already taken place at nearby Stockley Park, where a series of refined office buildings are surrounded by gardens and landscaped car parks. Increased land costs at Bedfont Lakes meant that higher density development was necessary, suggesting a solution that was more urban in style. Hopkins devised a regular, symmetrical plan where seven buildings stand around a square with gardens and a car park. The buildings, three storeys in height and 18 m deep, rise above the three levels of the sunken car park.

IBM, co-developers of the project, commissioned Hopkins to design three buildings at the northern end of the square. The result reaffirms the Miesian tradition of classic minimalism, construed as truth to materials, geometrical regularity and extreme refinement in its use of technology. The exposed steel frame offers great structural synthesis embellished with an innovative element: a nodal casting that links the beams and columns, tapering to accommodate the different dimensions of the columns, which diminish in size from one level to the next. The structural frame is infilled with glass and grey-painted aluminium panels, and fixed external louvre screens.

The main building, at the short end of the square, has a classic layout, arranged around a brightly-lit central atrium where the High-Tech character of the project: is evident; the roof, in fact, consists of glass panels suspended from the lattice trusses of the primary structure that covers the whole span (18 m) without intermediate columns; the ingenious glass-fibre fabric sun shades are also anchored to this structure.

The node of the distribution stands with monumental power in the centre of the atrium: an assemblage of lift shafts, bridges. A long straight staircases divides the floor space into two areas, one devoted to socialization, where there is a restaurant, the other occupied by the firm's marketing department. Accessible from a gallery, the offices are divided by glazed partitions to gain the maximum bright daylight from the atrium.

The same steel and glass façade is used in the two smaller flanking buildings, which have a fully glazed recess in the centre: this interruption indicates the entrance, while its transparency reveals an elegant spiral staircase.

Reference to the work of Mies van der Rohe is evident, in particular the Illinois Institute of Technology campus, which Hopkins visited while working on the project for the IBM building. The sense of space at Bedfont Lakes was clearly inspired by the classic monumentality of ITT buildings, like Mies's Crown Hall.

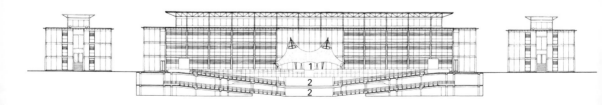

Section across site

1 management centre
2 staff parking

Opposite page
The glass covered atrium
and its circulation system

The special nodal casting

Ground floor plan

1 entrance to New Square
2 building entrance
3 customer centre
4 auditorium
5 dining
6 kitchen
7 offices
8 management centre
9 visitor parking
10 down to staff parking
11 lake

Opposite page
Building façade

Following pages
View from the regained
parkland

Glyndebourne Opera House
Sussex
1989–94

The chance to build a theatre devoted to performance of opera has, generally speaking, been a rare opportunity in Great Britain in the past century; it is no surprise that the project for a new theatre at Glyndebourne. attracted the attention of many of the nation's leading architects The Glyndebourne Opera Festival – which is the fruit of the Christie family's determination, and does not receive a grant from the Arts Council – runs from May to August, offering an intense opera season with a country house party atmosphere: during the long intervals members of the audience may visit the neo-Elizabethan house and the gardens, where traditionally they enjoy champagne picnics (complete with the classic hampers) on the grass, while the orchestra plays croquet.

Sir George Christie, in his role as a latter-day patron of the arts, sent the stipulations for the new project to Norman Foster, Robert Adam, James Stirling, Peter Ahrends, Sam Lloyd, Nicholas Thompson, Edward Cullinan, Richard MacCormac and Michael Hopkins, stating: "Glyndebourne is a country house that has generated a theatre. There is no need, however, for the new theatre to copy the style of either the house or the old theatre that has grown up in a casual and fragmentary manner over the last fifty years and today is nothing more than an example of the worst eclecticism. The new theatre must be convincing from a functional point of view, have identity and character but without offending public taste, ... I realize that what is described today as an 'architectural masterpiece' must to a certain extent have a 'signature', but the style of this 'signature' must be able to convince us in its first year of life as much as in the next hundred".

Romantic and pragmatic, technological and artisanal, functional and welcoming, exclusive and informal at the same time: this was what Sir George's new theatre had to be.

There was fierce competition between Michael Hopkins and James Stirling for the commission: the neo-Georgian theatre with 830 seats, built by Edmond Warre in 1932, would have to be demolished to make way for a world-class theatre seating about 1,200 people. Stirling's scheme involved the restoration of many of the existing buildings, manifesting the tendency towards small-scale fragmentation that is typical of the English countryside; Hopkins's project (the successful one) proposed, on the other hand, a single volume on an elliptical plan that reflected his continuing interest in the expressive potential of the circular form, already evident in the David Mellor Cutlery Factory and the Queen's Building in Cambridge: it was an imposing and innovative building that benefited from the skills of local craftspeople, updating them with the sophisticated engineering of Ove Arup & Partners.

The load-bearing structure consists of a double brick wall, separated by a 50-millimetre air chamber, forming a drum 33.7 m in diameter and 17.7 m in height. Resting on the interior elevation, are the auditorium roof, the stage wings, and the backstage; on the external elevation, the floors of the auxiliary spaces. This drum is truncated where it meets the fly tower, which is a freestanding steel and concrete structure. The auditorium ceiling is made with precast fair-faced concrete panels, as are the soffits of the balconies, the boxes, and the gallery. The panels supported on a series of circular columns are tied back into the rear brick wall and cantilever radially towards the centre where they are joined by a ring beaml.

These elements, especially the ceiling panels, play a fundamental role in the auditorium's acoustics and the insulation of the roof. Above the concrete ceiling, a metal structure supports a double layer of lead-covered plywood panels, thus continuing the double shell that characterizes the sound insulation of the walls.

In order to correct the focalization of the high frequency sounds caused by the circular form of the brick enclosing wall, the auditorium ceiling, in the form of a shallow cone, is surrounded by suitably calibrated and shaped vertical concrete panels; for the same effect the walls are linked with convex wood panels, while the balconies have specially curved fronts to reflect the sound from the stage. The seats combine a refined design with important technological devices, such as the ventilation system, where fresh air is delivered through their perforated metal pedestals.

An outer load-bearing structure of 185 linear m runs parallel to the first: on this fair-faced brick wall are the elevations that, in the part containing the ancillary spaces, are constituted by a continuous curtain-wall, while, in the public part, they are perforated by a two-storey arcade with two hundred flat arches giving onto the foyer. This structure consists of massive brickwork, a stretcher and a header in width, with flat arches having a span of up to 2.76 m, supported on both sides by piers 44.8 cm in thickness, tapering as they rise from a width of 1.18 m at the base, 79 cm at the

first storey, 56.2 cm at the second story and 22 cm at the third storey. The ends of the radially arranged concrete floor beams are visible in the piers: this is a significant detail making the composition of the structure legible, so that it becomes the aesthetic expression.

An artisanal and innovative construction that is, at the same time, solid and light, it aspires to the dematerialization of the brickwork, exalting its *gravitas*: this is a form of experimentation continuing that of Louis Kahn in the Phillips Exeter Academy Library, New Hampshire. But it also seeks to make the most of tradition and local crafts, which are particularly evident in the choice of bricks and mortar: the bricks, of the Alton type, are handmade in order to have the same size (22 x 10.6 x 6 cm) as those of the existing structure; the lime mortar consists of a mixture in use before the Second World War, which remains soft so as absorb the movements of the structure, eliminating any need for expansion joints. Thus, structural continuity is achieved,

enhancing the appearance of the whole building.

The polyester fibre membrane structure gives a summery feel to the setting and its formal and technical characteristics are well suited to forming the link between the new and the old. Thus it is modern, but, at the same time, closely linked to the nineteenth-century functionalist tradition – especially the tenets of Augustus Pugin – which lives again in the structural honesty and the unadorned sensuality of the exterior and interior, where brick, glass, wood and steel are juxtaposed, but not touching.

Devoid of stuccoes, hangings and curtains, the interior is enveloped by the warm amber colour of the pitch pine that transforms it into the ultimate musical instrument. Glyndebourne is an exercise in precision of execution, expressive honesty and tectonic minimalism similar to a Victorian industrial building where, however, past, present and future coexist in unique harmony.

Opposite page
View from park

Longitudinal section

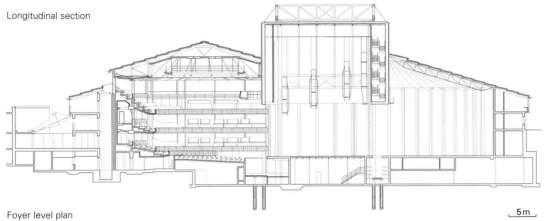

Foyer level plan

1 foyer
2 auditorium
3 orchestra pit
4 stage
5 backstage
6 sidestage
7 box office

5m

5m

Site plan

1 foyer
2 auditorium
3 stage
4 backstage
5 side stage
6 box office
7 bar
8 shop
9 organ room
10 rehearsal stage
11 loading bay
12 restaurant
13 car park
14 Mildmay hall

20 m

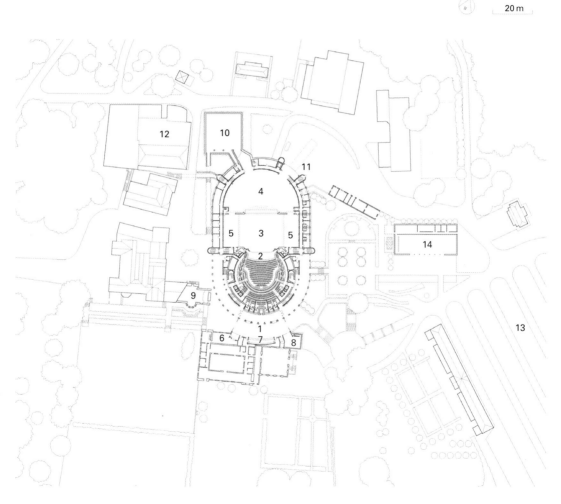

Opposite page
Approach from the garden

The fabric-covered foyer
in daylight

Opposite page
Backstage

Following pages
The auditorium as seen
from the stage

Chapter 3

Architecture of Technology and Materials: Consolidation of a Philosophy

"Form follows material" is the expression that best sums up the evolution of Hopkins's architecture in his mature period.

This is architecture that uses technology and materials to transform the radical High Tech of the early avant-garde into the innovative epilogue of the Modern Movement.

Since the 1960s, this has been a movement in search of an outcome: Hopkins rewrites its rules in a new language where tradition and modernity, memory and the contemporary world are but metacategories of time.

Workplaces
Inland Revenue Centre, Nottingham, 1992–95
Saga Group Headquarters, Folkestone, Kent, 1996–98
Portcullis House, New Parliamentary Building, London, 1989–2000
Westminster Underground Station, London, 1990–99
The Wellcome Trust Gibbs Building, London, 1999–2004
GEK-Terna Headquarters, Athens, Greece, 2000–03
Hälley VI, British Antarctic Survey, 2005
Shin-Marunouchi, Tokyo, Japan, 2001–07

Recreation
Buckingham Palace Ticket Office, London, 1994–95
Goodwood Racecourse, Sussex, 1997–2001
Hampshire County Cricket Club, Southampton, Hampshire, 1994–2001
Inn the Park, St James' Park, London, 1998–2004
Norwich Cathedral

Refectory Centre, Norfolk, 1995–2004
Alnwick Garden Pavilion, Northumberland, 2003–06
"Utopia" Broughton Hall, Yorkshire, 2001–05

Culture
Dynamic Earth, Edinburgh, 1990–99
Wildscreen@Bristol, 1995–2000
The Forum, Norwich, Norfolk, 1996–2001
Manchester Art Gallery, 1994–2002
Royal Academy of Arts, London, 2003

Education
Jubilee Campus, University of Nottingham, 1996–99
National College for School Leadership, University of Nottingham, 2000–02
The Pilkington Laboratories, Sherborne School, Dorset, 1995–2000
The National Tennis Centre, Roehampton, London, 1999–2007

The New Science Building, Bryanston School, Blanford, Dorset, 2002–07
Northern Arizona University Advanced Research and Development Facility, Flagstaff, Arizona, USA, 2003–
The Kroon Building, School of Forestry and Environmental Studies, Yale University, New Haven, USA, 2005–
Chemistry Building, Princeton University, USA, 2005–

Collegiate
Queen's Building, Emmanuel College, Cambridge, 1993–95
Lady Sarah Cohen House, London, 1993–96
Sheltered Housing, Charterhouse, London, 1994–2000
Haberdashers' Hall, London, 1996–2002

Health Care
Evelina Children's Hospital, London, 1999–2005
Ambulatory Cancer Care Centre, University London College Hospitals, 2005–

Inland Revenue Centre
Nottingham
1992–95

A major industrial city in the East Midlands, Nottingham was heavily bombed during the war, and rebuilt willy-nilly in the 1960s. Later, under the Thatcher government of the 1980s, it underwent a phase of indiscriminate speculative building. An important public structure, like the new offices for 1800 employees of the Inland Revenue, was, therefore, the ideal opportunity for starting the long-awaited process of urban renewal of the city.

The Treasury chose a site near the city centre: this was semi-derelict industrial land below the Castle Rock, bounded to the north by a canal and the south by a railway, where a start had already been made with a design-build project, which, however, the then Treasury minister was soon obliged to abandon due to the protests from both the professionals and the residents, who were concerned about the low quality of the design. In order to speed things up, a limited competition was held, with the participants including Richard Rogers, Michael Hopkins, Demetri Porphyrios, Evans & Shalev, Arup Associates, and Nicholas Hare. Hopkins's proposal won because he transformed a situation with tight limits on time and costs into an opportunity for an innovative project linking prefabrication to sustainable solutions with low running costs. The project had following aims: the extension of the urban grain of the city centre southwards; the improvement of the view of the castle; the creation of a flexible plan with a small-scale impact; the use of traditional materials, passive methods of energy production, and innovative construction methods in order to reduce times and costs of the building process. Hopkins proposed a clear and rational complex to be built using a structural system based on the assembly of prefabricated components that renewed the building process and allowed work to be completed in just one year. The scheme consisted of seven blocks with a regular layout divided along its east-west axis by a tree-lined boulevard-backbone, and intersected by three radiating streets (converging in the direction of the castle) that strengthen the relationship between the old and new parts of the city. The office space requested (430.000 sq m) is housed in two blocks with courtyards and four L-shaped ones, three and four storeys in height, centring on a glazed reception and amenity building, which is covered by a polyester fibre tensile structure anchored by a system of cables and masts. It houses a multi-purpose sports court, (bar, cafeteria, restaurant), meeting rooms, and a nursery for fifty The originality of the design for the amenity building becomes even more notable if compared to the rigorous standardization of the office blocks conceived as an assemblage of parts, sorting out structure and aesthetic in one powerful gesture as required by the best British Structuralist schools.

The structural framework consists of 1,032 prefabricated fair-face brick piers topped by precast concrete capitals bearing the precast concrete ceiling units: this building process is ground-breaking in regard to its precision, safety and speed of assembly on site. The piers, which taper as they rise, and the variable thickness of the shallow vaults of the ceiling units (28 cm at the edges, 12.5 cm at the tops of the vaults) create a geometric balance that gives a strong rhythm to the structure of the elevation, into which the smaller elements are inserted: this stylistic choice updates, with new technical methods, the dematerialization of the brickwork undertaken by Louis Kahn in the Philips Exeter Academy Library, New Hampshire.

The energy-conservation philosophy guides other design choices such as the width of the blocks, which is never more than 13.5 m so as to allow the offices to benefit from natural light and ventilation. The characteristic modular niches that give rhythm to the elevations are created by the full-height sliding windows fitted with external metal balustrades and semi-reflective glass light shelves over the windows that reflect light upwards to the ceiling.

A system of components and subcomponents transforms the building into an intelligent machine expressing the state of the art in bioclimatology: the piers and ceiling units constitute the thermal mass, the glass and steel are the elements that protect, light and ventilate the interiors. Ventilation is effected naturally with minimal use of mechanical plant: the air enters at the bottom and is removed at the top, its normal flow being produced by the heat gain resulting from the windows, people, and equipment. Fresh air is brought into the interiors of the offices through perimeter grilles and fan/heater units beneath the raised floors; as it heats up, it is drawn towards the stair towers with glass- block walls that serve as thermal chimneys. In addition to resolving architecturally the buildings' corners and containing the vertical circulation, the towers capture the hot air and expel it: an automatic mechanism that controls the fabric covered dampers on the rooftops, raising them by up to one metre, according to need.

An apparently simple building, it is, in reality, sophisticated, "intelligent", and assembled on site using industrial processes that put different traditional techniques on the same footing. The combination of ancient materials such as bricks with other more recent ones, helps create an innovative architectural grammar, which is attentive to such present-day issues as sustainability and develops a process integrating design, production, construction.

The precast brick piers

Lowering the precast
concrete floor panels

Aerial view showing site
below castle

Opposite page
Façade detail

The Amenity building for
sport and relaxation

Opposite page
The entrance at night

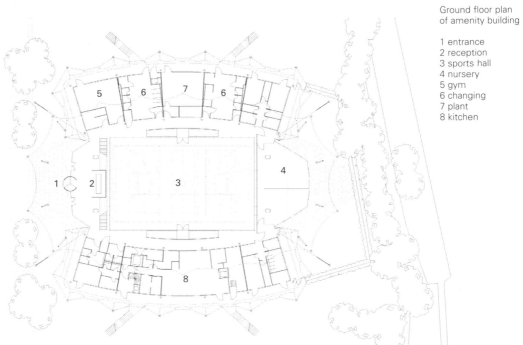

Ground floor plan
of amenity building

1 entrance
2 reception
3 sports hall
4 nursery
5 gym
6 changing
7 plant
8 kitchen

10 m

Workplaces
Saga Group Headquarters
Folkestone, Kent
1996–98

Unlike the business park at Bedford Lakes, the office complex built for the Saga Group, which sells vacation packages and financial services to the over-fifties, is located in an outstanding setting, occupying a hilly, 28-acre site sloping gently towards the English Channel, in the village of Sandgate, near Folkestone, Kent.

The site was formerly the grounds of Enbrook – a famous country house built in 1853 by Samuel Sanders Teulon in the Gothic Revival style for the Count of Darnley – then restored by Sir Edwin Cooper and listed Grade II in the early twentieth century. Because the house had been considerably altered, the authorities were persuaded to allow its demolition, providing the new buildings were of the highest architectural quality in harmony with the landscape.

Thus the environmental setting guided the choices of the new project. With what could be described as Wrightian sensitivity, the glazed volumes facing the sea frame the natural world that surrounds and penetrates the architecture: the vegetation, the sun, the wind, and the changing seasons continue to live inside the building, which, despite its radical High-Tech appearance, functions in harmony with the environment and its ecosystem.

The amenity building, known as the Pavilion, is available for use by the local community: its layout, already put to the test in the Schlumberger Research Centre in Cambridge and the Inland Revenue Centre in Nottingham, comprises a large central space flanked by two rows of secondary structures, which, in this case, consist of meeting and training rooms and a day nursery for the employees' children. The building has the dynamic profile of the tensile structure: the arches of the roof are supported by an asymmetric system of bicycle-wheel struts so that the arched windows which span the width of the hall all face the sea. The structure consists of tubular steel beams (diameter 32.4 cm, span 32 m) to which are attached glass-fibre membranes treated with polytetrafluoroethylene (PTFE). The design of this structure was further complicated by the need to develop appropriate technology for such details as the correct double curve of the fabric in order to prevent tearing under atmospheric loads and the execution of the joints between fabric, glass and steel so that they are waterproof but, at the same time, allow for the thermal movement of the different materials.

The exuberance of the Pavilion's forms, their concave and convex surfaces enhanced by the interplay of the vast canopies of the tensile structure, contrasts with the more sober and monumental office block: this is a five-floor building standing on a two-storey podium cut into the hillside and flanked by two glass towers.

The structure is a mixed system of round concrete columns, steel transverse beams, and precast floor slabs with exposed, vaulted soffits. As there are no suspended ceilings, all the services are located under the raised floors.

On the upper floor of the podium there is a courtyard covered by a roof garden overlooked by the glass curtain-wall of the office block. Its flexible layout can house a variety of functions, ranging from the open plan call-centre area on the ground floor to the executive offices on the top floor, from which there is access to a terrace with splendid views of the Channel; all the offices are located at the rear of the building so as not to obstruct the view of the sea.

The desire to protect the privacy of the building and keep it under control is evident in the decision to locate the entrance in a half-hidden position on the west side. This entrance gives access to a subterranean hall constructed with fair-faced concrete, from which an imposing staircase leads to an internal street bathed with the light filtering through the triple volume of the glazed atrium.

The atrium is an environmental buffer zone in the interior of a complex bioclimatic system: in winter, the large glazed surface accumulates passive heat; in summer, the natural ventilation cools the air, which is then distributed under the raised floors, where grilles allow it to enter the offices. Numerous plants transform the atrium into a conservatory, allowing the office windows to be opened even on cold or windy days. The glass wall is not, therefore, a barrier between the natural and built environments, but rather a sensitive screen that interacts with the exterior in order to regulate the microclimate of the interior.

The system based on low energy consumption is completed with the contribution of the two side towers, which, like those of the Inland Revenue Centre in Nottingham, help to ventilate the building: in this case the towers are crowned by two swivelling metal cowls that serve to expel the stale air thanks to the suction power of the coastal breezes.

This is a complex, therefore, that exemplifies the potential of contemporary architecture to implement sustainability through innovation.

A fabric covered central
Pavilion faces south
towards the sea

The two buildings are different in character but loosely related to one another

The atrium of the office block forms an environmental buffer zone to the offices

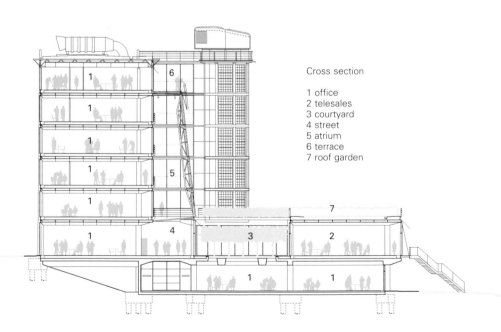

Cross section

1 office
2 telesales
3 courtyard
4 street
5 atrium
6 terrace
7 roof garden

5m

Workplaces
Portcullis House, New Parliamentary Building
London, SW1
1989–2000

After nine years of planning and two of construction, Portcullis House housing Committee Rooms and Offices for over two hundred MPs was finally opened. A shining example of the potential of innovative architecture, the scheme required leading British architects and engineers to solve the problems of the site's setting and structural constraints posed by the exceptional context – where such monuments as Big Ben and Westminster Bridge combine history and institutions in a synthesis that is unique in London – and the requirements of the London Underground Act (1992), calling for the renewal and extension of the underground network with a new District and Circle Lines station under the Palace of Westminster's foundations, and a new Jubilee Line station and tunnel along the perimeter of the site.

Thus the plan for modernizing the underground network excluded all the initial proposals for the renovation of the nineteenth-century buildings on Bridge Street and Victoria Embankment, and instead favoured a solution involving demolition of the old buildings to make room for the new parliamentary building and the underground station below, conceived as two distinct entities that were, however, to be structurally linked.

After approval by the Cabinet on 9 March 1992, the final plan set out the following objectives:
– a Parliamentary Campus in the block bounded by Bridge Street, Richmond Terrace, Victoria Street and Parliament Street;
– a network of links (courtyards and passageways) between the Houses of Parliament and Portcullis House providing internal circulation for the security of the MPs;
– a courtyard layout in order to take full advantage of the site's surface area and allow natural lighting of the offices;
– ancillary facilities (such as restaurants and reading rooms) serving the buildings on the north side (the Norman Shaw buildings) with access from the courtyard;
– a new building in harmony with the urban context, especially such pre-existing edifices as the Norman Shaw buildings.
The result was a seven-storey block built round a covered courtyard: on the ground floor there are restaurants and shops; on the first floor, meeting rooms and libraries; on the five floors above, the MPs' private offices.

The layout is simple, paradigmatic in its division between "served" and "servant" spaces. Following the canons of High-Tech, the building's complexity is lent a hierarchical order by its structural elements, which are assembled with the classic constructive minimalism that enhances the materials' performance and expressive qualities. The rigorous harmony of tensions and clear equilibria denotes an architectural system consisting of the following components: stone piers, precast concrete "gull-wing" floor units, bronze fixtures, patinated aluminium bronze roofing, suspended concrete corner structures, precast concrete arches with the function of transferring loads, a grid of laminated oak beams for the courtyard roof, and the mechanical plant.

The originality and innovative character of Portcullis House's loadbearing structure derives from its coordination with Westminster underground station situated below: the pillars along the perimeter walls rest on a substructure of the station, while the inner piers in the courtyard transfer the load onto the arches that, in their turn, discharge it onto the six columns of the station's loadbearing structure.

The traditional floor system of beams and pillars consists of prestressed sandstone pillars, precast "gull-wing" units – their shape deriving from the pattern of the isostatic forces – occupying the whole width of the building (13.8 x 3.6 m); their thickness varies from 12 to 25 cm and they weigh 35 tonnes. The façade is animated by the rhythm of the fair-face concrete arches, containing aggregate that glitters like marble in the sun, and the tapering Birchover stone piers – resting on Dartmoor granite plinths – that progressively taperstorey by storey, from 120 x 60 cm at the first level to 50 x 60 cm at the fourth level.

This structural system develops techniques already put to the test in the Glyndebourne Opera House and in the Inland Revenue Centre in Nottingham, which was being built when the project for the new parliamentary building was already underway. The system of tapering piers and arched floor units adopted in Nottingham has, however, a substantial structural difference: the brick piers can react to torque, while the stone piers of the parliamentary building can only be subjected to traction and compression because the building is devoid of a loadbearing structure at the corners. The corner towers – with the exception of the north-west one, where the mechanical services and

the water supply for cooling are located – are, in fact, suspended from a transfer structure anchored to the trusses on the seventh floor.

The roof, with its groups of eight bronze and steel box girders, extending – four on each side – down the slope of the roof for three storeys and described as "spiders' legs", is topped by fourteen chimneys that continue the profile of the roofs of the neighbouring Norman Shaw buildings; their size is due to the need, given the lack of a basement, to house the ventilation plant in them. The ventilation system, in fact, plays a fundamental role in the planning and design of this building. The quest for an architectural language that also expresses the ethics of sustainable building has long been one of the overriding concerns of Hopkins, who aims to combine form, structure and bioclimatics in a global aesthetic.

Low-energy plant assists systems such as that of the "fat façade", which exploits the thickness of the external wall in order to insert ducts for the circulation of air: the bronze-clad ducts are placed on the façade between the piers and the bay windows, a strategic position that allows the section of the ducts to expand upwards in inverse proportion to the tapering of the stone piers, reflecting the increased need for fresh air on the upper floors.

The rooms are ventilated in the following way: the fresh air is drawn in through the grilles on the bases of the chimneys; a thermal wheel stabilizes its temperature before it is circulated through ducts in the external walls to the plenums under the raised floors, from where it enters the rooms through floor grilles. The exhaust air enters the return ducts through inward projections of the light shelves, emerging from the cowls on the tops of the chimneys. This system of air circulation recalls the arterial and venous system of the human body: its heart is the enthalpy wheel that pumps, cools and heats the air. Subcomponents such as triple glazing, solar screens and Venetian blinds help keep the building cool in the summer and prevent loss of heat in the winter.

Hopkins has continued the revival of traditional materials with the conception of piers in pre-stressed stone that lend mass and texture to the design of the building and lightness and economy to the construction.

In the courtyard, the classic fabric tensile structure, a Hopkins trademark, is replaced by a spectacular glazed roof, notable for its technical and spatial refinement: the tops of the six loadbearing columns bear prefabricated pads from each of which spring four struts supporting the diagrid of Canadian oak laminated beams, anchored to the string-course capitals of the internal elevation and constituting the loadbearing framework of the barrel vault consisting of triangular panels of tempered glass, linked by spherical stainless-steel joints.

The construction of Portcullis House involved a very complex process that required constant electronic monitoring of the loads in order to ensure that the safety limits were not being exceeded, especially with regard to the asymmetric loads on the arches.

British efficiency and pragmatism allowed this building of great technical precision to be realized without, however, neglecting its sensitivity to the context: the Norman Shaw buildings are echoed by the tall ventilation chimneys and rounded corners, just as the Palace of Westminster's Perpendicular Gothic is reflected by the building's verticality and the materials of its façade, as well as by the conception of the loadbearing structure, which may be described as Gothic in its poetic equilibrium of suspended and linking tensions.

The High-Tech phenomenon thus reaches its maturity with a project that has the power, syntactic rigour and human and urban scale of the greatest classicism, updated with innovation that manifests faith in the ethics of sustainable building and links structure, function and expression in an integrated process.

Exploded isometric

1 members and plant
2 members and staff
3 members and staff
4 committe rooms and
conference facilities
5 courtyard
6 Parliament Square
7 Palace of Westminster

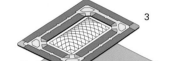

Opposite page
Façade detail

The new Parliamentary
offices occupy one of the
most prominent building
sites in the country

Panel of light reflectors
suspended from the glass
courtyard roof

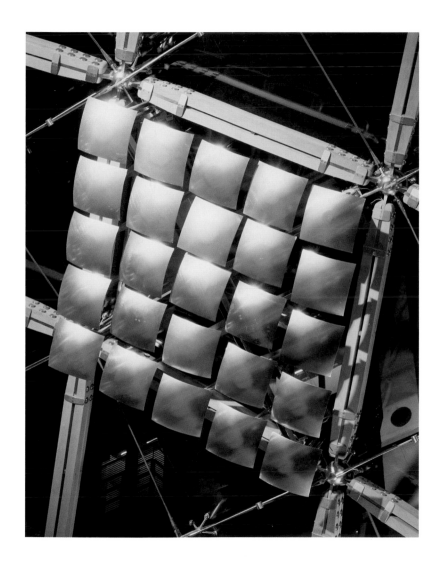

Section showing the
environmental strategy

1 exhaust air
2 exhaust air fan
3 services distribution rack
4 supply air handling unit
5 façade air shafts
6 fresh air in
7 thermal wheel

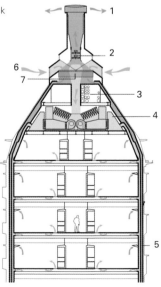

Bay window detail

1 bronze façade
2 lightshelf
3 precast structural slab
4 extract plenum
5 blind within window
cavity
6 bench seat

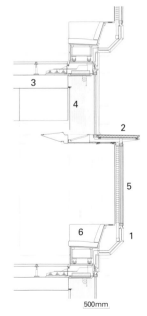

500mm

Façade detail next
to Big Ben

Westminster Underground Station
Westminster, London, SW1
1990–99

The realization of the new Westminster underground station, which became the interchange between the District and Circle lines and the Jubilee Line extension, was possible thanks to the integrated planning of the structure of the station and the Parliamentary Building over it.

A special order of the Ministry of Transport permitted the demolition of the building previously standing on the site so as to allow the creation of a structural system able to meet the requirements of the new complex: the solution adopted provided for an arched structure with the function of transferring the loads and the lowering by 30 cm of the tracks of the District and Circle lines in order to allow the ticket hall to be inserted between the platform level and the ground floor of the new Parliamentary Building.

The project for the new station consists of the reconstruction of the operational parts, the building of the new ticket hall, new platforms and imposing escalators, built inside a structural box measuring 72 m in length, 22 m in width and 30 m in depth.

On the upper level, the District and Circle lines cut diagonally across the site, which meant a three-dimensional structure was needed to support the levels above the pre-existing configuration of the tracks. The box containing the lifts and escalators was inserted in this structure.

The enormous structure was designed in order to counteract the earth pressure of the ground surrounding the excavations for the foundations of the new Parliamentary Building.

The construction of the station will be remembered as an incredible success of twentieth-century civil engineering, executed in a particularly congested and delicate area of the capital and requiring a total of six years to build.

The interior sparkles due to the choice of the aggregate in the concrete, which includes micaceous iron powder and marble chips, while the grey of the fair-face concrete is repeated on the austere perforated steel panels used for the screens and balustrades.

Exploded isometric view

1 courtyard
2 District & Circle Lines
3 escalator box
4 Eastbound Jubilee Line
5 Westbound Jubilee Line

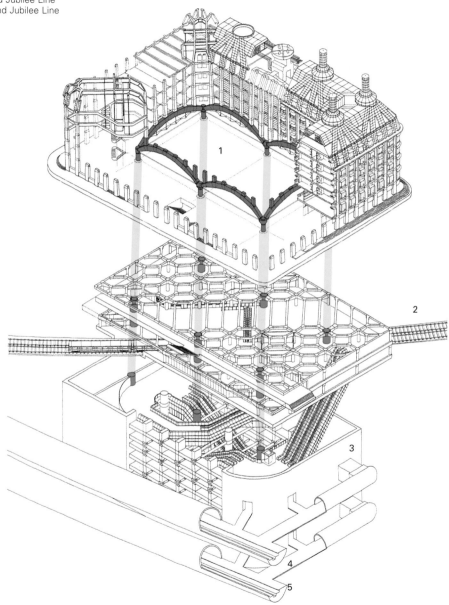

Opposite page
Into the Piranesian interior
of the underground station

The Wellcome Trust Gibbs Building
Euston Road, London, NW1
1999–2004

Founded by Henry Wellcome in 1936 and internationally renowned for its contribution to the Human Genome Project, the Wellcome Trust is one of the most important independent charities supporting the biomedical sector, funding about twenty per cent of research in this sector worldwide.

Designed to accommodate the Trust's six hundred staff, previously spread over five sites in the Euston area, the new building (known as the Gibbs Building) occupies the site on the corner of Euston Road and Gower Street with a single compact volume, comprising two blocks divided by a large atrium between them. Despite its independence and apparent lack of relation to the context, the new building has kept a link with Wellcome's neighbouring building, which, constructed in the 1930s in Neo-Classical style, is being refurbished to house the Trust's library and art collection, both open to the public.

Situated in a central area of London, near Euston Station and the University College London, the building's forms respond to the architectural tradition of its context: the north block, on the busy traffic artery of Euston Road, is ten storeys high, but the south block, facing the much quieter Gower Place – where the urban fabric is reduced in intensity and scale – has only five storeys. The gentle curve of the roof joins the two blocks with their differences in level thanks to an innovative structure of steel and glass covering the atrium, which is spanned by walkways linking the two blocks.

Without seeking simply to fit in with the styles of the neighbouring buildings – consisting of the old Wellcome Building and the early nineteenth-century forecourt of University College – the project takes into account the impact of its own volume on them. The building, which is otherwise symmetrical, is cut back on the Gower Street corner to allow improved access to the Euston Square underground station.

Thus the new building is conceived as two office blocks separated by a large atrium forming an internal "street" 90 m in length: this is a clear, functional structure, enhanced by refined design, ranging from the technological details and the rigorous coherence of the plan and the elevation to the bioclimatic strategies applied to the steel and glass construction.

The clear composition of the Euston Road elevation of the north block echoes its equally simple internal arrangement: each floor is divided into five column-free open spaces, each 12 by 18 m and divided by mini-atria two storeys high. These five spaces are reflected on the façade by five glazed bays separated by four recesses, the outer two of which contain stair towers clad in glass blocks, while the inner two accommodate the exposed steel cross-bracing.

The south block, which is narrower, has an equally rigorous elevation: this is a fully glazed façade concealing four floors of offices; the top floor houses the staff restaurant, which commands splendid views across Bloomsbury.

The structural frame of the building is of a mixed type, in steel and concrete: reinforced concrete columns and sheet metal and in-situ concrete floors. Most of the building is faced with glass panels (3.4 x 3 m) that not only have an aesthetic function, but also form an advanced system for its bioclimatic conditioning. The panels consist of a single layer of glass, an air space of one metre with internal mechanical louvres and then two layers of glass: as well as allowing access for maintenance, the wide insulating layer serves as a climatic filter – it is, in effect, a ventilation duct that cools the air, ejecting it from the vents on the roof. An advanced monitoring and automatic control system establishes the energy demand for the conditioning of the interior, thus avoiding waste of resources. This is an innovative concept of energy control that allows us to look optimistically towards a future of sustainable buildings.

Not only is this a building with a strong identity and urban presence, but, in its Euston Road elevation, it also reflects the horizontal division of the façade of the old Wellcome Building into base, column and attic; the notable verticality of its elevation is a further tribute to the Giant Order of the adjacent Neo-Classical building.

Cross section

1 main entrance
2 staff entrance
3 office
4 bookstore
5 restaurant
6 atrium
7 plant

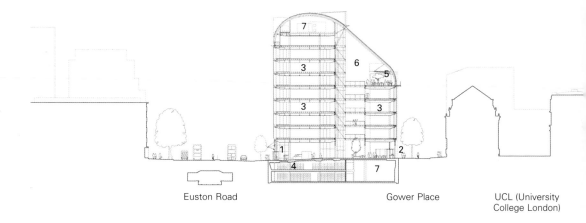

Euston Road   Gower Place   UCL (University
                                                     College London)

Typical upper floor plan

1 office
2 mini-atrium
3 link
4 library
5 reading room
6 reading room

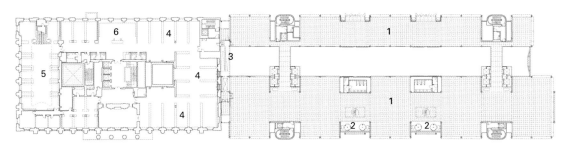

6m

View within the atrium

Opposite page
View above the atrium

Entrance façade detail
at night

Workplaces
GEK-Terna Headquarters
Athens, Greece
2000–03

In 2000 the Greek construction company GEK-Terna organized a limited international competition for its new Athens headquarters, inviting Michael Hopkins, the Swiss Luigi Snozzi and the Portuguese Eduardo Souto de Moura to participate. This trio of names is itself an indication of the objectives of the scheme. The winning feature of Hopkins's design is that of having ingeniously resolved the relationship with a hostile setting: Mesogion Avenue is a six-lane arterial road linking Athens to its new airport, lined for about ten kilometres by speculative commercial buildings.

The corner site, which has the form of an irregular rhomboid, is fully exploited, obtaining a total of 11,000 square metres of useable space in two perimetric blocks opening fanwise, with the circulation and service cores at the narrow end. The courtyard layout creates a private microcosm protected by the two wings of the offices. The two compact blocks have continuous frontages on the busy Mesagion Avenue and the quieter Kalamon Street, allowing the courtyard to take the form of an urban square, with the functions of facilitating interface between the personnel and regulating the internal climate in the hot summer months.

The layout highlights spatial themes familiar in Hopkins's architecture, such as arcaded access, circulation with a gallery, and the services and circulation at the ends of the blocks so that "served" and "servant" spaces are clearly separated.

In the courtyard, glass panels line both the office walls and the parapets of the gallery, although horizontal louvres interrupt this visual permeability. The interiors are designed to make the most of the materials and skills of the Greek craftsmen: wood finishes and concrete structures enhanced by moulded profiles are made according to the best local building procedures.

Although this is an area with many planning restrictions, Hopkins was able to design a building that could fit into its urban setting and, at the same time, create the parameters for a prototype to be used for other office blocks.

As usual, the building reveals its structural features, consisting of the grid of primary structures (6 x 6 m) of in-situ concrete to which all the substructures are linked, including the mesh of steel rods, cut horizontally by the wooden handrails that are a feature of the internal façades.

The GEK-Terna building follows in the footsteps of such urban projects as Bracken House and Portcullis House. Design choices remain essentially the same whether in Britain or in the Mediterranean: choices rooted in sustainable design to build an architecture that even in its complexity remains clear and readable in all its parts.

Isometric view

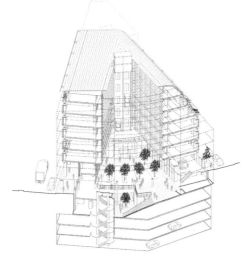

Opposite page
The façade on the residential street

Ground floor plan

1 entrance
2 reception
3 courtyard
4 office
5 café
6 arcade

5m

Cross section

1 office
2 atrium
3 arcade
4 café
5 multi-purpose hall
6 car park

Opposite page
View of the open courtyard

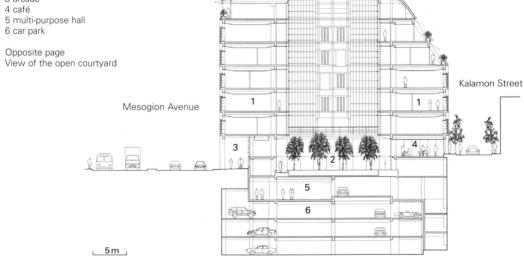

5m

A working terrace

The lower level
of the courtyard

Opposite page
Looking across
the courtyard

Workplaces
Hälley VI, British Antarctic Survey
2005
competition

Halley VI is a scientific research station for the British Antarctic Survey: this project is a tremendous challenge because of the environmental restrictions to be overcome and the aims of the competition brief:
– the design of a sustainable prototype suitable for the environment of the Antarctic where wind and snow are decisive factors;
– reduction to a minimum of the environmental impact during the lifecycle of the station, which must be constructed in accordance with the Environmental Protocol to the Antarctic Treaty;
— overcoming of the constrictions of the site, with the design of a structural system where the operations relating to the assembly, maintenance and relocation of the station will be reduced to the indispensable minimum;
— creation of a stimulating place to live and work with, at the same time, adequate flexibility to adjust to any changes of functions and users – at the moment, the design proposal caters for a staff of 16 people with the possibility of accommodating up to 52 extra residents in "couchette" type fold-down bunks in the 36 summer rooms.;
— reduction of risk factors through scientific planning while still seeking innovation;
— the design life of the station is at least twenty years, during which time it may need to be relocated to different sites kilometres apart;
— the project must be completed, commissioned and handed over to BAS by 31 December 2008.

This is a fascinating project to which Hopkins brings his vast store of experience, as well as his capacity for imagining the future, exploring and exploiting the potential of technology transferred from sectors other than the building industry: this is a challenge that recalls the beginnings of radical High-Tech, addressed today with the down-to-earth approach of an architect accustomed to conducting research into the practical applications of technology.

The design suggested by Hopkins/Expedition/Atelier Ten consists, therefore, of two buildings (pods), conceived with the logic of on-site assembly of components, one the operative base for the research activities, the other the accommodation and mess facilities. To minimise drift formation, container pods are elevated above ground of about 4 and 4.5 m. The buildings can be moved as frequently or infrequently as necessary thanks to a system of hydraulic legs that allow them to step up and walk across the ice shelf. The site itself is part of a moving masterplan that contains an engineered infrastructure.

The guiding concept in the development of this project is maximum efficiency combined with speed of construction: the aim is to create a simple structure and a flexible internal space. The buildings will be an assembly of prefabricated ISO containers (6.1m long x 2.44 m wide x 2.9 m high), fully fitted out before shipment, and arranged on two storeys. The structural system is a rigid modular framework of lightweight elements bolted together; the external cladding consists of a triple-skin inflated EFTE membrane with a high insulation capacity that – together with the building's ground clearance – provides an excellent system for snow drift management, as well as having the advantage of allowing a view of the exterior for continuous monitoring of the station and the surroundings.

The prototype has been designed to move over the snow on steel legs driven by hydraulic jacks (similar to those used for raising bridges) operated from within the building.

Halley VI is an ambitious project that foresees, in the long term, zero emission of CO_2, thanks to the wind-driven turbines, the production of energy from hydrogen and fuel cells. At present, however, this technology is still in its early stages, but, in any case, waste material will be reduced to a minimum, with recycling techniques and reuse of the materials and resources.

This is architecture of environmental engineering that aspires to create efficient and comfortable spaces in an extreme climate, inhospitable for man. It uses innovative technological strategies but keeps risk factors under control with the updating of tried-and-tested technologies rather than the invention of ones specifically for the new environment.

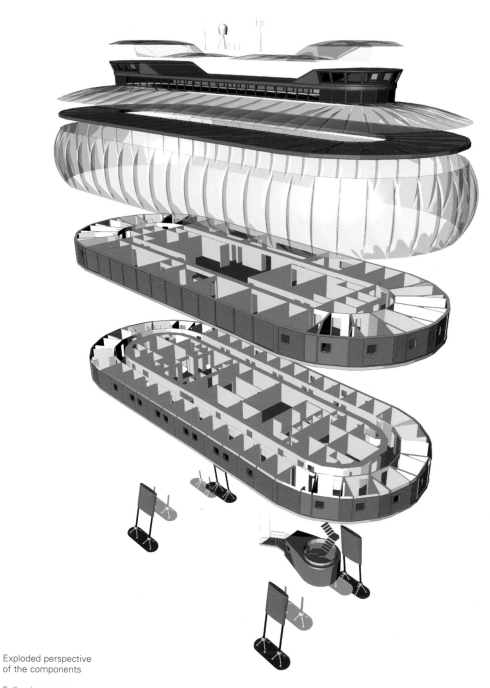

Exploded perspective
of the components

Following pages
Visualisation of the station
in its environment

Shin-Marunouchi
Tokyo, Japan
2001–07

In 2001 the Mitsubishi Estate Group, which manages the real property of the Mitsubishi Corporation, Japan's largest general trading company, commissioned Hopkins Architects to design an office, retail and restaurant development in the Marunouchi district of Tokyo. This is a prestigious assignment that confirms the office's international expansion after the commissions in Greece, Dubai and the United States.

The site is located in one of the city's leading business districts: the Tokyo Station Plaza, known also as the "gateway to Japan", from which an avenue leads to the Emperor's Palace.

The commission required a mixed-use complex with large stores, luxury boutiques, restaurants, and offices for international business tenants; it will be linked below ground level to the Tokyo Plaza metro station. The structure will be divided into two towers of different heights rising from a six-storey podium. The urban and intrinsic value of the project is revealed by the lightness of the volumetric relationships, the meticulous care taken over the details, the Miesian classicism of the structure that uses relationships on both the urban and human scales.

Steel and glass are, once again, the form and the contents, the container and the structure of the architecture of Hopkins, who, here too, demonstrates his great skill in resolving the relationship between architecture and its context.

Entrance foyer

An important site close to the Palace on Station Plaza

Recreation
Buckingham Palace Ticket Office
London, SW1
1994–95

Every summer, when the Royal Family are away, about 250,000 people visit Buckingham Palace; they buy their tickets from a little building on the edge of Green Park, facing the Queen Victoria Memorial and, beyond this, the palace itself.

Put up in August and taken down in September, this is a temporary pavilion consisting of three main components: a timber deck to protect the ground, a cabin to house the ticket sellers and a fabric canopy to shade and shelter the waiting queue.

The whole structure curves gently to follow the line of the curved balustrade between the road and the park: this is one of the many features revealing the attention paid to the details that, in this case, are an expression of belonging to a place. Built with the constructive precision of a boat, the cabin, which is 15 m in length, is a wooden structure with birch plywood ribs and horizontal cedar boarding. The corners are rounded with carved quadrant spheres, top and bottom, thus creating a smooth, continuous envelope. In order to preserve its reddish brown colour, the wood has been finished with yacht varnish.

The fabric canopy advertises the presence of the ticket-office, lending a note of summery cheerfulness to the building. At the ends, the acrylic canvas membrane is supported by laminated spruce masts linked through steel plates to laminated horizontal beams and a series of struts placed at intervals of 3 m. The acrylic membrane is attached to the struts, which are guyed by steel cables to the ground.

In this small-scale temporary structure, where a major role is played by technology, the architect's passion for materials and their techniques of assembly allow him to find the best possible compositional solution

Cross section

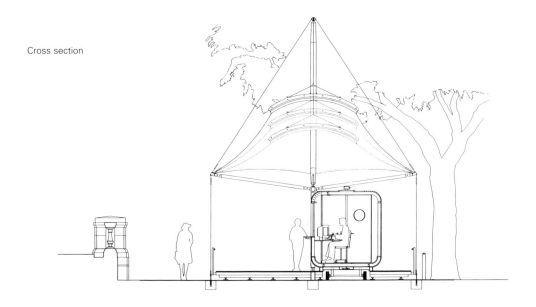

Recreation
Goodwood Racecourse
Sussex
1997–2001

The Goodwood Racecourse is located in the Goodwood Estate, belonging to the Dukes of Richmond who, since the nineteenth century, have promoted horseracing at a national level. Surrounded by the undulating hills of the South Downs, the racecourse commands splendid views, towards the south, of Chichester and the Isle of Wight.

In order to respond to the strong competition from the other sports and cultural events in the corporate entertainment market, Goodwood decided to improve the quality of its facilities by upgrading and extending the old racecourse. The new project focussed primarily on changing the function of three key spaces: the winner's enclosure, the parade ring, and the weighing-in building behind the main grandstand.

The axial sequence of these three elements still worked well, but the weighing-in building obstructed the promenade from the parade ring to the grandstand. The new layout, therefore, takes advantage of the lie of the land – which slopes down on the south side – to create a terraced mound with seating for the spectators; the weighing-in building and winners' enclosure now stand at a lower level than the promenade.

A new weighing-in building forms part of the retaining structure of the terraced mound, its roof at the level of the promenade. A fully glazed wall faces the winner's enclosure: this is a simple in-situ concrete structure with a flat roof slab supported on round columns. The jockeys' changing rooms are at the back of the building, while the stewards' offices and the BBC room are at the front. Stepped spectator stands extend from the side walls of the weighing-in building around the parade ring: this layout allows the promenade to be remodelled as a boulevard flanked by mature trees. At its west end this boulevard crosses the horsewalk – which links the parade ring to the racecourse – and meets the new tree-lined entrance road with a turning circle and drop-off point, thus forming a clearly legible circulation spine across the site.

Having established the new layout of the site and its circulation spine, it was necessary to design the catering and hospitality facilities, which are accommodated in three marquee-like structures covered by a PVC membrane supported by white-painted steel masts. A fourth tent shelters a pair of wooden cabins housing the ticket office and a meeting room.

By moving the entrance, a site to the west of the grandstand was made free: an elegant restaurant with champagne bar has been built here. Similar in form and structure to the weighing-in building, it overlooks the members' lawn and horsewalk.

The garden-party effect – the racecourse is only in use from May to September – is underscored by the wooden board flooring and the absence of perimeter walls in the pavilions, apart from, in the two outer ones, free-standing glass screens shielding spectators from strong southerly winds.

Site plan

1 entrance pavilion
2 parade ring
3 winners' enclosure
4 concourse
5 stables
6 racecourse
7 stands

N

50m

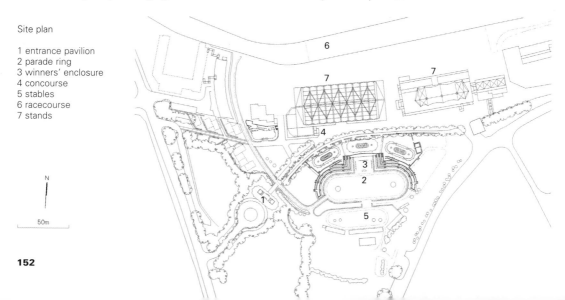

Racegoers at on
the Parade ring

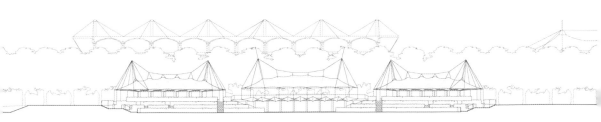

15m

Section through Parade ring

Pavilions enhance
the Parade ring

Recreation
Hampshire County Cricket Club
Southampton, Hampshire
1994–2001

When complete, the new cricket ground will comprise seating for at least 10,000 spectators, press facilities, the members' pavilion, hospitality suites and parking for 1,300 cars, as well as a cricket academy for young people wishing to improve their performance in the sport.

The elegant membrane structures of the pavilions are Hopkins's distinctive trademark and, here again, they lend lightness and structural dynamism to the whole complex. The steeply sloping site has been levelled to form an oval field surrounded by an earth bank, on the top of which stands a double line of trees, creating a sense of enclosure for the spectators and forming an excellent acoustic barrier from the noise of the nearby M27 motorway.

The new cricket ground is but part of a larger masterplan for the whole area, including a nine-hole golf course, an indoor bowling green, and a tennis club, which, together with the cricket club will make this one of the main sports and leisure centres in the Southampton area.

Site plan

1 match ground
2 nursery ground
3 pavilion and cricket
academy
4 nursery pavilion
5 seating terraces
6 entrance pavilions

50 m

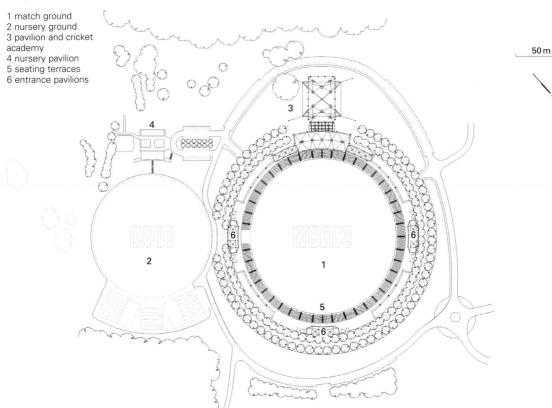

Section

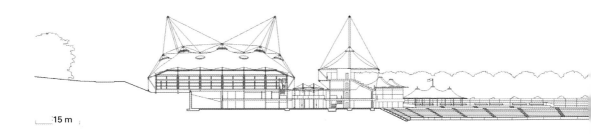

15 m

Inside the cricket nets

Recreation
Inn the Park
St James' Park, London, SW1
1998–2004

John Nash planned St James' Park in the picturesque style to emulate Nature's spontaneity, using soft slopes and gentle curves to create a meticulously detailed landscape. Hopkins takes his inspiration from Nash's sensitivity, designing the park's café as an ergonomic structure immersed in the greenery up to its rooftop; the only division inside is a band of glass offering views onto the Broadwalk and the lake. A grassy hillock rises up over the restaurant, insulating the building to keep it cool in the summer and warm in the winter. Along the edge of the roof terrace there is a promenade that may be reached by a flight of wooden steps.

The lowest part of the Broadwalk is contiguous with the terrace, which in turn leads into the wood panelled interior of the restaurant, all smoothly flowing. The more formal space of the restaurant opens gently out into the exterior.

The floorplan comprises an open space where round, wood columns define the different zones in the space: service, tables, terrace. The kitchens, toilets, storage and staff areas are located in a reinforced concrete box buried in the hillside.

The back wall follows the curved line of one of the paths, while the one in front all but vanishes in a glazed façade emphasizing the building's relationship with the park's landscape. This architecture is sunk into the landscape, where interiors and exteriors blend together perfectly in organic symmetry.

Ground floor plan

1 existing path
2 terrace
3 restauran
4 kitchen
5 existing stores
6 stairs to broadwalk

N

1 0m

The café sitting comfortably
within its landscape

Dining in St James' Park

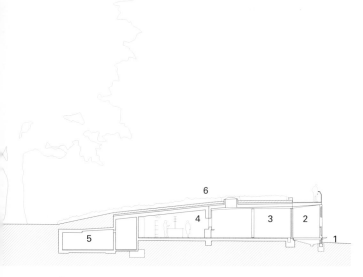

6

4   3   2

5   1

4 m

Section

1 foot path
2 terrace
3 restaurant
4 kitchen
5 stores
6 planted roof

The café has become
a popular meeting point

Recreation
Norwich Cathedral Refectory Centre
Norfolk
1995–2004

At Norwich Cathedral two new spaces were created along the south and west walls of the medieval cloister. The new architecture plays on old and new, with a radical solution that engages the original building while respecting its historic value: this ability characterizes Hopkins in his work on both *grands projets* and projects on a smaller scale.

The building work was to be realized in two separate phases: a cultural centre for exhibitions and conferences and a visitors' centre with a restaurant.

The first phase is complete, a new Cathedral Refectory replaces the original monastic refectory with a contextually inspired project developing the themes that explore the relationship between space and technology, history and modernity. Conceived as one space within another, the new refectory grows up within the ancient walls. The walls become a shell containing a technologically advanced timber structure of two stories.

The project is inspired by a constructive logic that connects the ancient walls to the new intervention, reconciling the contextual relationships with the pre-existing structures. Here, technology no longer serves merely as an instrument for carrying out the construction, but also as a method for updating architectural spaces. Thus, an existing fissure in the medieval wall can become the restaurant entrance, emphasizing the technological contrast between the weightiness of the masonry and the lightness of the iron, glass and wood structures of the stairs and lift, whose design is elegantly detailed by a Master from the best English structuralist school.

The texture of the materials, their solidity, transparency, lightness and colour are the defining elements of the project that balances high technology and craftsmanship, innovation and tradition.

The ancient 12th-century flint rubble walls are complemented by Clipsham stone surmounted by glass panels with chamfered louveres of untreated oak ; deep eaves with a lead gutter delimit the lead-clad pitched roof. The interior is very bright, thanks to entirely glazed gable ends. The space seems carved out of wood: the scheme offers two rows of slender laminated oak columns that rise out of hardwood floors, conferring fluidity and rigour upon the space. Each column terminates in a steel node supporting four struts that reach up to the wood-faced substructure of the roof. The structure combines old and new, making minimal impact on the medieval fabric, while supporting the heavy roofing with minimal apparent effort.

The structure is designed to give its components autonomy and lightness. Precise juxtapositions bring them to life, giving a sense of geometric solidity and exalting the qualities of the materials used.

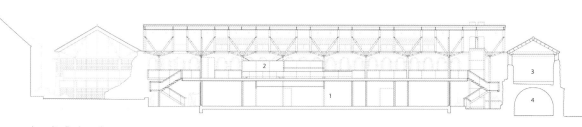

Longitudinal section

1 kitchens, toilets, stores and plant
2 restaurant
3 reading room
4 Dark Entry to cloister

5 m

Opposite page
Night view of refectory

Original perspective view

Site plan

1 cathedral
2 cloisters
3 hostry
4 refectory
5 Upper Close

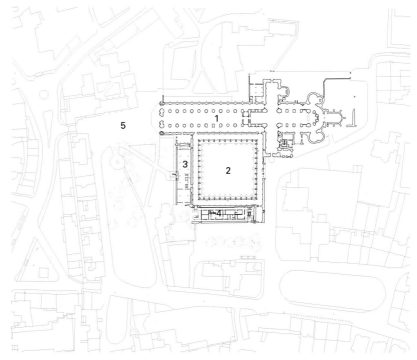

N

50m

First floor plan

1 servery
2 refectory
3 reading room
4 library entrance
5 library
6 hostry

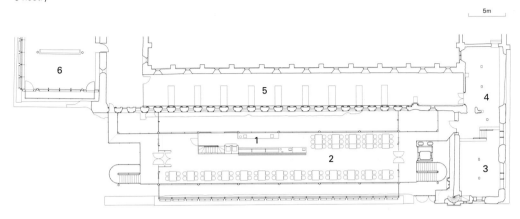

Ground floor plan

1 offices
2 kitchen
3 store

4 toilets
5 plant
6 south cloister
7 The Dark Entry
8 hostry

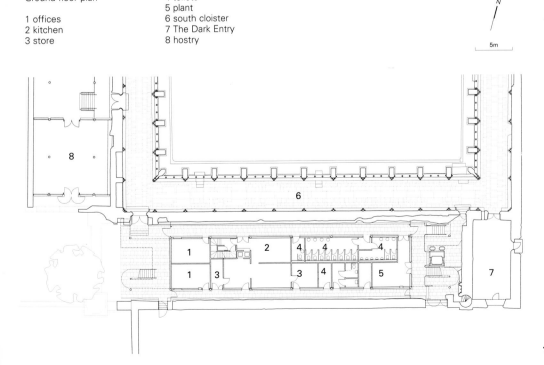

View of entrance

Interior view of refectory
with cathedral in the
background

Opposite page
Entrance detail
emphasising the meeting
of old and new materials

Opposite page
The new cast lead roof is
cantilevered towards the
cloister wall, but avoids
loading on the fabric

Recreation
Alnwick Garden Pavilion
Northumberland
2003–06

The Duchess of Northumberland commissioned Michael Hopkins to design the new visitor centre at Alnwick Garden, where the Dukes' medieval castle is located.

An expression of the art of English gardens, this open-air museum-park is one of northern England's major tourist attractions, with expected arrivals of 400,000 visitors every year. The 12-acre terrain theatrically landscaped by Capability Brown has been modernized by Wirtz, a Belgian landscape architecture studio, using the latest technology in garden design. The result is a park that is mindful of its origins yet worthy of the 21st century, where nature and the spectacular come together in fountains, ornamental labyrinths and thematic gardens.

Due to the popularity of the garden, it was clear that expanded visitor facilities, where tourists receive their initial orientation to the garden, and the creation of a large car park were needed.

The Hopkins project proposes two new structures: the Pavilion, located within the garden wall, and the Courtyard Building, outside. Although they are separate, the two buildings are closely linked through their design so as to constitute a single centre with related functions.

In the planning, the first objective was to confer a theatrical spaciousness upon the complex: think of the Pavilion as the orchestra facing the stage (the Garden), where Nature performs. The Courtyard Building, which develops in three sections around a courtyard, is a hypothetical foyer, with areas for social events and restaurants.

The Pavilion is a building on two levels where visitors may stop and eat: on the underground level are the kitchen, offices, restrooms and equipment; on the first floor, two restaurants (250 seats each) overlook the Garden.

The Courtyard Building is a single volume, consisting of a body with a rectangular plan and two lateral wings arranged around a central court. It houses education and reception services: admissions and orientation, the bar, retailing facilities, two cinemas with seating for 150, two conference rooms, restrooms, and the north-facing terrace.

The architectural strategy in terms of structure and detail is the same for each edifice, and both were designed with sustainability in mind, seeking maximum energy savings in terms of both construction and maintenance.

The building's structural framework is timber, and consists of perimeter columns supporting a diagonally oriented timber lattice barrel-vault. The rigorous floor plan is matched by the spectacular achievement of the roof: a triangular weave of laminated wood beams and cables with steel nods supporting the roof cladding that consists of an opaque system in some areas and a transparent skin in others. Conventional solid, isulated cladding system can be adopted in the opaque areas while inflated EFTE cushions would suit well the transparent areas. The walls are either glazed or made of aluminium panels and allow maximum visibility over the landscape. Most of the glass panels can be opened, allowing the rooms to air naturally, but also, and more importantly, giving fluidity and flexibility to the spaces, which are conceived in continuous dialogue with Nature both within and without.

Section

1 pavillion
2 protected wall
3 shop
4 education

5m

View of the new pavilion
from the cascade

View of pavilion from
the garden

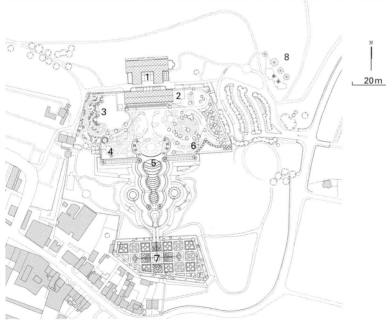

Garden plan

1 visitors' centre
2 pavilion
3 rose garden
4 serpent garden
5 cascade
6 poison garden
7 ornamental garden
8 tree house

20 m

Section

1 ETFE pillow
2 timber spars
3 fixed glazing
4 timber column
5 sliding door

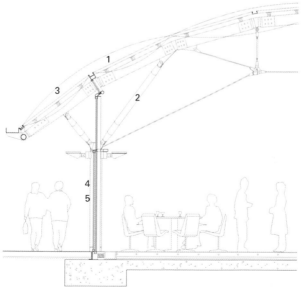

Recreation
"Utopia" Broughton Hall
Skipton, Yorkshire
2001–05

The new Pavilion provides an attractive communal facility at the centre of the Broughton Hall estate in north Yorkshire, which is run as a rural enterprise business.

Broughton Hall, altered in the nineteenth century to its present imposing form, is built out of local stone, set amidst 3000 acres of parkland. The surrounding listed, redundant out-buildings have been progressively converted to provide modern office accommodation for up to fourty businesses, who employ more than five hundreds staff.

There was a need for a communal building on the site to act as a central focus, providing a large common room, rooms for meeting and presentation and an area for lunch and evening events, with associated catering and service spaces.

An ideal site was identified at the top of the former walled kitchen garden, which had fallen into disuse. It has a commanding view over the remodelled garden to the surrounding countryside. The new single storey Pavilion sits confidently on its timber plinth, a contemporary yet natural building.

Entrance is across an open veranda, which surrounds the Pavilion. The central common room has frameless glass, front and back, and is flanked, symmetrically by timber clad "book ends", housing the smaller rooms, whose structure incorporates the laminated timber columns that support the roof – a clear– span steel truss, with a central roof light. Overhanging eaves shade the windows and protect the veranda with its outside seating area and graded steps leading to the garden.

Floor plan

1 entrance ramp
2 common space
3 meeting room
4 kitchen
5 servery
6 verandah

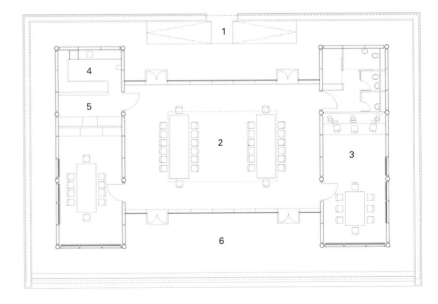

2m

A single storey pavilion set
within the former walled
kitchen garden

Cross section
1 entrance ramp
2 common space
3 verandah

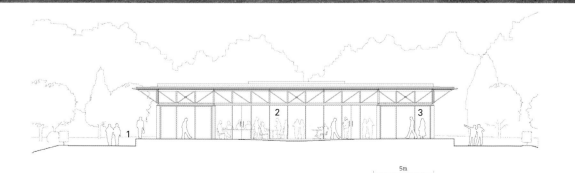

Opposite page
Looking out over the
kitchen garden from
common room

View towards large
common room

Overhanging eaves shade
the windows and protect a
continuous perimeter oak
verandah with steps
leading to the garden

Dynamic Earth
Edinburgh
1990–99

Dynamic Earth is an interactive museum where visitors may explore the planet, from the Big Bang to the latest cosmogonic theories. It is also a poetic expression of a recurrent theme in Michael Hopkins' architecture: the relationship between Nature and Artifice.

The material quality of the heavy sandstone and granite construction echoes the uncontaminated natural setting of Arthur's Seat and Salisbury Crag, and contrasts the light technologies of iron and glass that support the tensile fabric roof created through laboratory research. Nature and artifice, craftsmanship and industry, tradition and innovation: these recurrent dichotomies are the extremes of dynamic balances resolved through pure geometry and a passion for constructive authenticity, transforming even this project into a solution offering *gravitas*, an expression of the "tectonic tradition of Modern Architecture", to paraphrase Kenneth Frampton.

Edinburgh is known as the Athens of the North because of its history that is impressed in the solid and secure masses of its architecture and the wild strength of its landscape. This is the backdrop for the exercise in static equilibrium performed by the tensile fabric roof as it appears to float between the earth and the heavens.

Set against the cliffs of Salisbury Crags and nearby Holyroodhouse, the building develops along the east-west axis of the Royal Mile: a context steeped in memories and tradition. To this may be added the fact that the new museum rises up where, over 200 years ago, James Hutton, the father of modern geology, formulated his theory on rock formation.

Thus, when the old Scottish and Newcastle Brewery dismantled its plant, ceding the old structure to the City on condition that it be developed for public use, it was suggested that a museum be built there. And in that museum, the history of the Earth — as told using modern geology interacting with the virtual reality of events such as volcanic eruptions, earthquakes and the Big Bang — could be celebrated.

Financed in part by funds from the Millennium Commission, Dynamic Earth is comprised of three main structural parts: the "black box", the amphitheatre, and the tensile fabric roof and its structure.

The brief called for a "black box", or a flexible container to house multimedia exhibitions and a planetarium: while the architectural potential seemed limited, the site offered vast possibilities. Hopkins suggested revising the shell of the old factory in the interest of an archaeology that, as in the projects for the Mound Stand and the David Mellor factory, is recognised as having current value, in the name of a "continuity" that now finds strong public support. The old Tudor masonry was restored and expanded to create the shell of the museum's two floors that would become a microcosm of the history of Edinburgh and its relationships with geology and the history of Mankind.

The load-bearing stone walls are stabilised by an internal structure with a grill of round columns supporting smooth or coffered reinforced concrete slabs.

A hemispherical dome bursts into the "box", like a sphere emerging from the floor to indicate something below: on either side is a spiral stair, one for entry and the other for exit, leading to and from the exhibition space on the two floors below.

On the stone foundation rises the transparency of the glazed walls of the entry marking a union of old and new. This is dominated by the tension of the fabric tent (PTFE): lightness, suspension, permeability — achieved using advanced technologies — symbolise Man's involvement with Nature. The masts that pierce the covering seem to reach towards the infinite. The taut, pointed, asymmetric corners of the fabric hail Nature, unpredictable and dynamic, and already way beyond the rationalistic and mechanistic theories of the old Newtonian world.

The local tradition for public spaces is revisited in the structure of the museum forecourt: an amphitheatre where performances and the annual Edinburgh Festival, in particular, are held.

Nature and the construction, memories and current issues, transparency and solidity cohabit in a boundless synthesis.

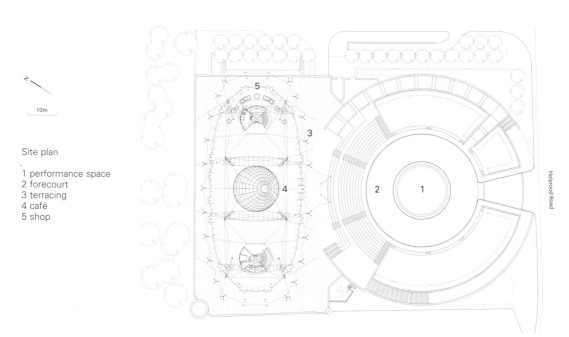

N

10m

Site plan

1 performance space
2 forecourt
3 terracing
4 café
5 shop

Holyrood Road

Dramatic view at night

Section

1-2-3
exhibition space with
dome

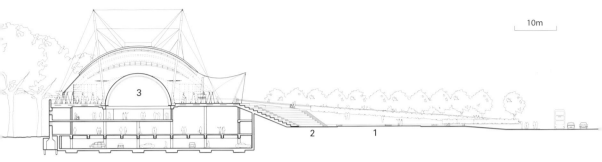

10m

3

2   1

Following pages
Interior view

The terrace ramparts
give spectacular views

Culture
Wildscreen@Bristol
1995–2000

Wildscreen@Bristol is part of a larger plan to revitalise Bristol's old Docklands area that involved the creation of an interactive museum centre and improving the surrounding area. The initiative represents an ambitious educational and leisure programme for the city with areas for stopping and eating within a theatrical urban setting of sculptures, fountains and water features, created in part thanks to funding from the Millennium Commission.

Opened in 2000, Wildscreen is an interactive centre targeting younger users, who are invited to participate in the cognitive process through contact with the latest technologies. A planetarium, an electronic zoo, a tropical greenhouse, and an Imax cinema revealing Nature's mysteries can all be found within the five-part complex, bordered to the north by Anchor Road and to the south by the nineteenth century Leadworks building. These include the 350-seat IMAX cinema, the foyer, the "black box" exhibition space, the botanical house, the ancient Leadworks. The scheme is thus an exercise in the aggregation of new spaces with the integration of existing old buildings.

The Leadworks was converted by gutting the interior, which was redesigned to accommodate modern offices for the administration; what remains is the nineteenth-century shell, now with a stretched teflon and fibreglass (ETFE) covering anchored to it, establishing the space of the foyer where the museum's ticket area is located. This solution reflects the one used at Glyndebourne theatre, and there are other compositional and structural similarities between the two buildings. Joined to the botanical house by a glass wall, the volume of the IMAX is in fact a masonry drum. It has an outer shell made of full brick masonry, and an inner one made of cement blocks lightened by two rows of iron girders. The foyer leads into a vaulted gallery in light-coloured concrete with recessed spotlights that guide the visitor and highlight its geometry. The fluid space of the foyer, covered with the soft forms of the fibre, draws up to and contrasts the clean, geometric exposed concrete volume of the gallery. The materials thus make it possible to read the different spaces of form and function.

The imposing curved façade of the IMAX dominates the end of the gallery. The structure's two layers of masonry are separated by an air chamber providing acoustic and thermal insulation. The interior "box" is made of concrete blocks, while the external drum is made from brick headers. The roof is constructed with radial steel trusses with a suspended ceiling for acoustic purposes.

The IMAX is connected to the tropical garden by elevated passageways made of glass blocks supported by profiled steel girders. The greenhouse is covered by a minimally-structured transparent ETFE pillow envelope that works like triple glazing. The pillows are supported by tension cables anchored to tie-beams that distribute the weight to two load-bearing raking masts that perforate the covering, to be exposed externally, in best High-Tech fashion. Working with transparency and solidity, with combinations of pure, minimalist, unembellished materials, Hopkins creates a compositional synthesis, which respects the character and authenticity of each individual part. While it is a bare brutalist matrix that brings the thinking of A.W.N. Pugin to mind, the radical High-Tech theory of-kit architecture also re-emerges. This architecture is thus like a series of themes to be re-elaborated and perfected from both the aesthetic and constructive points of view.

Section
1 IMAX theatre
2 link
3 bar
4 vault
5 tropical house
6 foyer
7 shop
8 cafè
9 offices
10 electronic zoo
11 exhibition back up
12 education
13 terrace

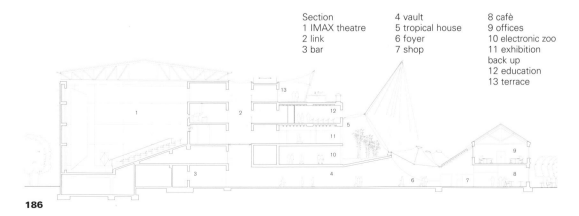

Ground floor plan

1 link
2 bar
3 vault
4 tropical house
5 foyer
6 shop
7 cafè

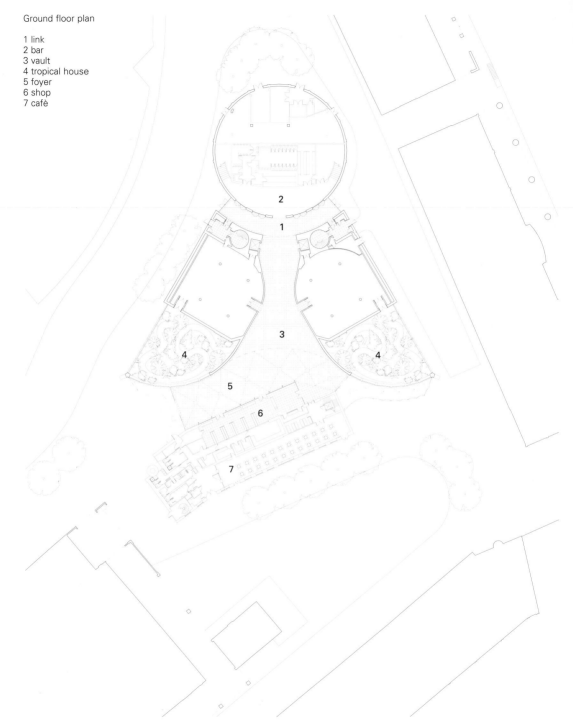

The entry vault to the
exhibition

Axonometric of complex

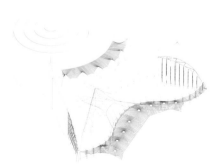

The membrane roof
of the tropical house
is suspended by a pair
of raking masts

Culture
The Forum
Norwich, Norfolk
1996–2001

The Forum is a public initiative, involving a site in Norwich's historic centre, surrounded by some of the most important civic buildings: City Hall, the Theatre Royal, the Assembly Hall and the gothic church of St Peter Mancroft.

When Norwich Library was destroyed by fire in 1994, the City of Norwich and Norfolk County Council decided jointly to build a centre of knowledge, information and learning. Here, the cultural and social life of a wide territory would be resurrected in a major new information hub at the disposal of the entire county. The new centre was inaugurated in 2001, and, thanks to its architectonic value, it was sponsored by the Millennium Commission.

The scheme combines the old Library site with the adjacent car park to form a city block along Bethel Street. This recurrent design shows Hopkins' preference for mono-volumetric solutions springing from clear floor plans with sharply-defined served and service spaces. Thus, a clear architectural design solves the urban and typological complexity inherent to the mix of functions: library, business and learning resources centre, restaurant, and regional BBC TV and Radio broadcast studio.

The volume is a play of geometry and materials that brings together disparate forms and textures in a powerful design. Concavity and convexity, transparencies and solids are the features of a horseshoe-shaped plan that is divided into three principal units: an apse, two naves and a central atrium that embraces the exterior, thanks to an entirely glazed façade that is illuminated in the evening, casting light over the modern *civitas*.

The main entrance is emphasized by a recessed glass wall that reflects the church of St Peter Mancroft opposite. The church acquires a new parvis in the form of the square called Millennium Plain, which is characterised by tiered steps that resolve the change in quota (3 m) while simultaneously conferring a monumental identity upon the new city centre. The public functions are housed behind the main façade which is glazed to better interact with the city, while the private functions are located in the apsidal section, protected by the massive brick structure. Inside the powerful semicircular drum is the library with 220 study stations. The spectacular façade is a glazed wall set between two brick towers, enclosing the atrium, which has the feel of a covered city square, and all the dynamism of the upper floors revolves around this open space.

The semicircular west side houses the library on all three levels: on the ground floor, a glass screen acoustically insulates it from the atrium while visually connecting the two spaces; on the first floor, a platform is inserted into the volume where it appears to float; the double volume of the first floor is split by the circular gallery set back on the second floor where reading spaces are located. The café and the restaurant area develope along a raised pathway connecting the two side aisles in a solution that breaks up the imposing volume of the atrium with a space full of vitality and social interactivity.

The rectangular wings contain: on the first floor, spaces for encounters, including a cafeteria, bookshop, and information centre. While these are independent spaces, they remain in view since they are separated only by a "skin" of glass; on the second floor are the more private functions, with the archives and the library collection to the north and a business centre to the south.

The symmetry of the complex is broken up by a semicylindrical volume that fits into the southernmost façade like a second apse. This structure has a 200-seat multimedia theatre and in the basement of this is housed the Heritage Visitor Attraction. The complex has a two-storey underground car park with 200 spaces. The roof of the Forum is supported by tubular steel bow-string trusses with zinc-covered metal decking infilling the pointed ellipses formed by these tubes, while the adjoining areas are glazed.

According to the new imperatives of sustainable innovation, the project adopted an energy saving building strategy. The key sustainable strategy consists of thick walls and the greenhouse effect of the glazed atrium; its windows let in light and may be opened for natural ventilation. The atrium and the hallways are paths for air circulation, and are naturally cooled by the mechanism of the enthalpic wheel and air treatment units. Lightweight technology using steel and glass combines with the procedures for heavy construction, and is punctuated by a regular rhythm of windows. As on other occasions, the bricks used were moulded expressly (in this case 19 mm longer than standard bricks), to create the curved and straight geometries of the new building, as well as to harmonize with the stairs of the old City Hall facing it.

The language is based on a grammar that has been perfected over time: circular form, design of the constructive details, planimetric distribution, volumetric unity… and their strength lies in their being the most natural solution to complex problems. The materials are minimal, expressed with constructive honesty and structural logic based on the hierarchical role of the components within the complex technological system. This project is innovative both in its use of original building solutions and its modern application of traditional techniques, as in the use of brick.

First floor plan

1 library
2 BBC radio studios
3 BBC TV studios
4 BBC newsroom
5 restaurant
6 retail

Bottom
Model view of the
development within
its urban context

Opposite page
Detail of the façade
of the brick drum

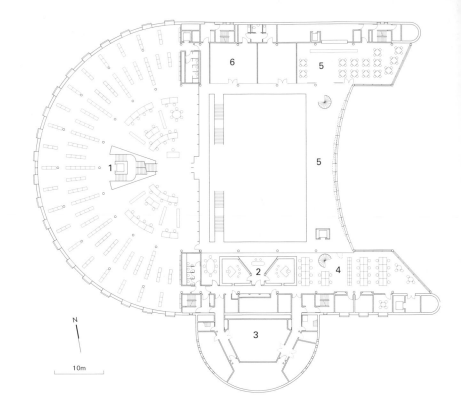

N

10m

Manchester Art Gallery
1994–2002

In 1994, the City of Manchester held an international competition for a new city art gallery. The brief required reusing two existing buildings and expanding them with a new construction to occupy the part of the site that was being used as a car park.

The existing buildings are two architectonic expressions of the city, built in the nineteenth century by Sir Charles Barry, the architect of the House of Parliament. They are the neo-classical Royal Manchester Institution and the Athaeneum, a Palladian-style gentlemen's club whose original proportions altered by a neo-baroque volume in the attic storey following a fire in 1873 and subsequent gutting.

From 1882, the Royal Manchester Institution was home to the Art Gallery. In 1938 the city acquired the Athaeneum in order to create a single museum centre, but this scheme was not be realised until the beginning of the Third Millennium, almost 100 years later.

The area to be built on, bisected by Back George Street, which flows between the two existing buildings, is located within the original Georgian fabric of Manchester. Hopkins redefines the edges of the block and creates a new art centre by conservatively repairing Charles Barry's work and creating a new building to increase the exhibition space from 900 to 2500 sq.m.

The project is an exercise in delicate contextualism carried out within the logic of rigorous functionalism: the existing organisation remains essentially unchanged, with the rear façade expanded by a new block dividing it into three symmetrical segments marked by concrete and glass cylindrical towers. These allow vertical distribution and echo the tripartite ABABA scheme of the existing nineteenth-century building.

A glazed, frameless space joins the two buildings along the Back George Street axis: the transparency integrates the spaces while maintaining the different levels of history. This link generates a second entry and an atrium occupied by the new grand staircase and two towers for lift access to the new rooms, which reflect the dimensions of the existing rooms to maintain spatial continuity.

The existing ionic portico remains the main entry. It leads into the double volume of the atrium while a grand staircase leads to the exhibition rooms: on the first floor, a gently sloping ramp also leads to the extension, in a fluidity of spaces that joins the old and the new in harmonious solutions.

The shop, coffee bar and restaurant, the education department, loading dock and the Manchester Gallery, which illustrates the history of the city, are all located on the ground floor. Storage, offices and archives are located in a basement. Training and conference rooms are located on the ground floor of the Athenaeum.

The intervention thus respects the historic context, and retains axial alignment and symmetry: such references in no way upset the identity of the new architecture that proposes a clearly autonomous and readable language.

This structure is made from pre-cast concrete elements (made off site) which are then carefully bolted and joined together on site.: The gallery floors are held up by huge precast architectural quality concrete vaults: curved slabs are a recurring components of Hopkins' buildings for both formal and utility purposes, taking advantage of the design to house the lighting fitting. In this instance, translucent panels act as filters to avoid harsh illumination of the paintings.

The steel frame of the glazed atrium constitutes the load bearing structure for the floor panels, the stairs, the ramp and the wall covering. Every single component of this structure is suspended from above, giving the principal structural elements the nickname "trapezists"!

To emphasize its role as extension, the new block is faced with bronze-framed stone panels that protect the ventilated façade.

After the urban planning, Hopkins had to work with the monumentality of the civic classicism of the Victorian period. This architecture was regulated by proportions, ornaments and typologies with a tight range of expressive codes that Hopkins contrasts with a neutral aesthetic of mute façades and minimalist glazed passages that transmit a philosophy of understatement well suited to exalting the innovative value of the new urban reconstruction.

Section through glazed link

1 main entrance hall
2 existing galleries
3 shop
4 glazed link
5 atrium
6 art lift
7 temporary exhibition
gallery
8 new gallery

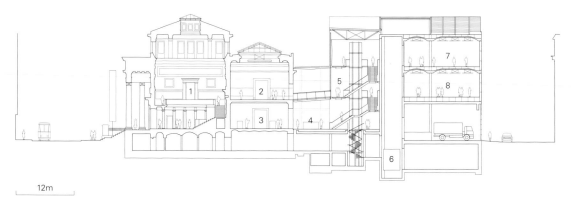

12m

Ground floor plan

1 entrance hall
2 shop
3 Manchester Gallery
4 café
5 atrium
6 works on paper
7 multi-functional room
8 classroom
9 art lift
10 loading bay

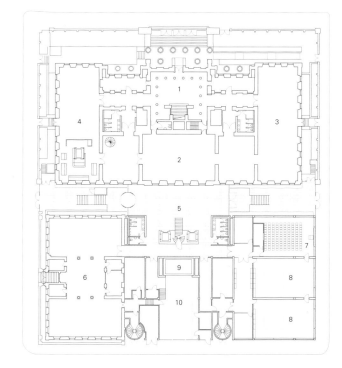

10m

First floor plan

1 main entrance hall
2 existing galleries
3 glazed link
4 atrium
5 Athenaeum gallery
6 new galleries
7 art lift

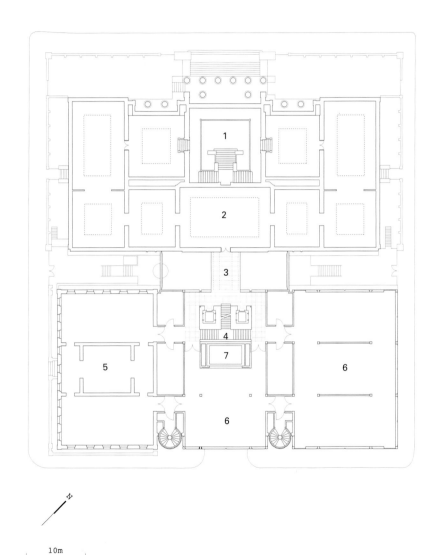

10m

View of the new galleries

Opposite page
The entrance connecting
the old and new building

Culture
Royal Academy of Arts
London
2003
project

Finding new ways of using ancillary areas, and re-ordering the non-gallery public spaces brings a new coherence and vastly improved visitor facilities to the Royal Academy.

The Royal Academy has some of London's grandest spaces designed by some of Britain's finest architects. But, dating from different periods and many being designed for different purposes, they were absorbed piecemeal as the Academy grew. Our proposals bring an overall order to this complex of buildings, devising new routes and connections which allow the finest spaces to reach their potential, and making better use of the ancillary areas.

The spur is the Academy's imminent purchase of 10 Burlington Gardens, a grandiose and unforgiving Victorian pile with a chequered history and large galleries which will give the Academy space to expand its educational and architectural departments. Connecting Burlington Gardens with the existing Academy will be a fabric-roofed space which will house a restaurant in what is now an unattractive lightwell over the Schools Corridor. This is the highlight in a re-ordering of the ancillary spaces below the public galleries and the courtyard and entrance hall, modifying these elegant spaces so their character is not overwhelmed by the demands of a modern museum. Visitors will enter via the cleaned and re-paved courtyard with a gently cambered ramp leading to the entrance into the hall, which, with ticket desks recessed, will be more spacious.

Re-opened arches under the main staircase will lead to a bookshop, from where a bridge will spring to the new restaurant. Without touching the existing galleries, the Academy will have enormously enhanced facilities, which will allow it to play a larger role in London's cultural and public life.

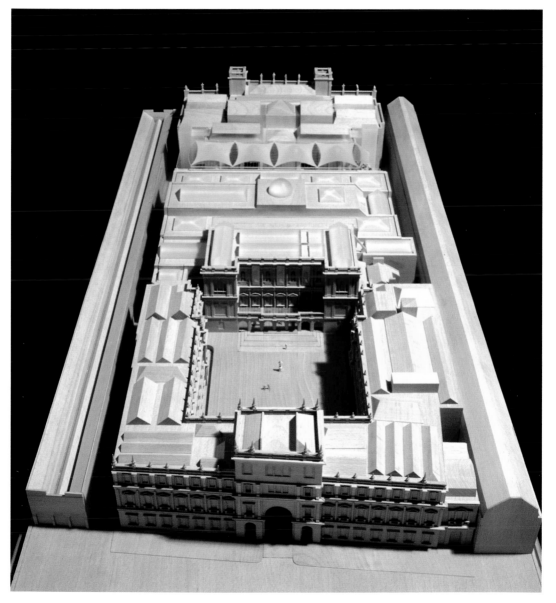

Jubilee Campus, University of Nottingham
1996–99

The University of Nottingham celebrated the centennial of its foundation with the inauguration of a new campus for 2,500 students that includes three departments, Economics, Computer Sciences and Sociology, a central library, two residence halls, and a congress centre (The Exchange) with three auditoriums, seating 100, 200, and 300 respectively.

Located next to a post-war residential zone, the Jubilee Campus occupies a lot on the edge of Nottingham's industrial area, formerly the Raleigh bicycle factory site, demolished to reclaim 7.5 hectares of land.

The project proposes the usual rational layout tempered by a romantic landscape emphasizing the relationship between the buildings and nature. In keeping with the best English tradition, the landscape is lushly planted and includes an artificial lake (13,000 sq.m.) conceived as a bioclimatic screen between the new campus and the city.

The property runs buildings follow the line of the lake offering a view to each of the faculty blocks with their central atria, as well as to the conference hall and the crescent of graduate students' residence halls. The undergraduates' residence halls, instead, have a more traditional courtyard arrangement, to the southeast of the lot.

The academic buildings have simple and economical structures: they are three storeys tall with rectangular plans, and offer the advantage of flexible spatial solutions. Hopkins proposes a lakeshore path that winds through the buildings' ground-floor arcades: a promenade running between nature and artifice, alternating gardens and permeable glazed atria that offer a glimpse of busy student life. Designed as semi-outdoor spaces, the atria, which are relatively narrow, are planted with trees and have informal furnishings. But above all they play an important role in the bio-climatic strategy: their covering of single-layer glass panels and the absence of heating turn them into greenhouse heat storage systems in the winter.

The visual fulcrum is the library, which breaks up the rational rhythm of the building layout with a volume in the shape of an upside down cone floating on a polygonal platform, connected by a short causeway to The Exchange conference centre.

The interior, like New York's Guggenheim, displays the continuous unwinding of a spiral ramp along the building's perimeter and leading to four floors of reading rooms. The structure is a reinforced concrete grill of girders and columns; it has Canadian red cedar cladding and wood frames with galvanised steel profiles.

One of the plan's primary objectives is to take advantage of the building's orientation to make use of an energy saving policy. Sustainable building concepts take advantage of strategies such as: the thermal mass of cement, roof gardens and screen-devices on the façade (retractable awnings and sunshades). The cedar strips, which over time will acquire a silvery grey colour, make an attractive cladding for sandwich panels using a new insulating material made of recycled paper (Warmcell): the system is called the "breathing wall" for its high rate of transpiration.

As in the Saga call-centre, the new Parliament building, and in the nearby Inland Revenue Centre, air cooling is based on the use of wind. Cool south-west breezes, further cooled by the lake, are captured by the grills of solar chimneys and passed through the electrostatic filters of the air handling unit (AHU) located on the roof; they are then directed down vertical ducts into floor plenums, to be distributed via a system of floor vents.

Exhaust air is channelled along the corridors and directed by diffusers towards stairwell towers, whence it is extracted by the rotating oast-house cowls on solar chimneys.

A thermal wheel inside the air-handling unit recuperates heat from exhaust air in the winter. Energy for the units is provided by wind and, when necessary, by photovoltaic cells inside the glass chamber of the panels covering the congress centre atrium and producing 51,240 KWh per annum.

In this way the atrium becomes a generator of energy, a source of light, and the "heart" of campus social life.

Hopkins created a university centre consistently sustainable down to the last details: an innovative centre that succeeds in updating the language of a traditional material such as wood, both in its constructive conception and in its formal expression

The former bicycle
factory site

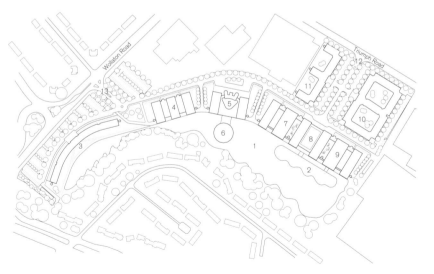

Site plan

1 lake
2 grassed island
3 post graduate hall
4 Business School
5 central teaching facility
6 Learning Resource Centre
7 department of Computer
Science
8 central catering facility
9 departments of education
10 undergraduate Hall A
11 undergraduate Hall B
12 entrance
13 main entrance

100 m

View of pedestrian
colonnade on front
of building

The Learning Resource
Centre and conical lecture
halls

1 lake
2 Learning Resource
Centre
3 100 seat theatre
4 200 seat theatre
5 300 seat theatre

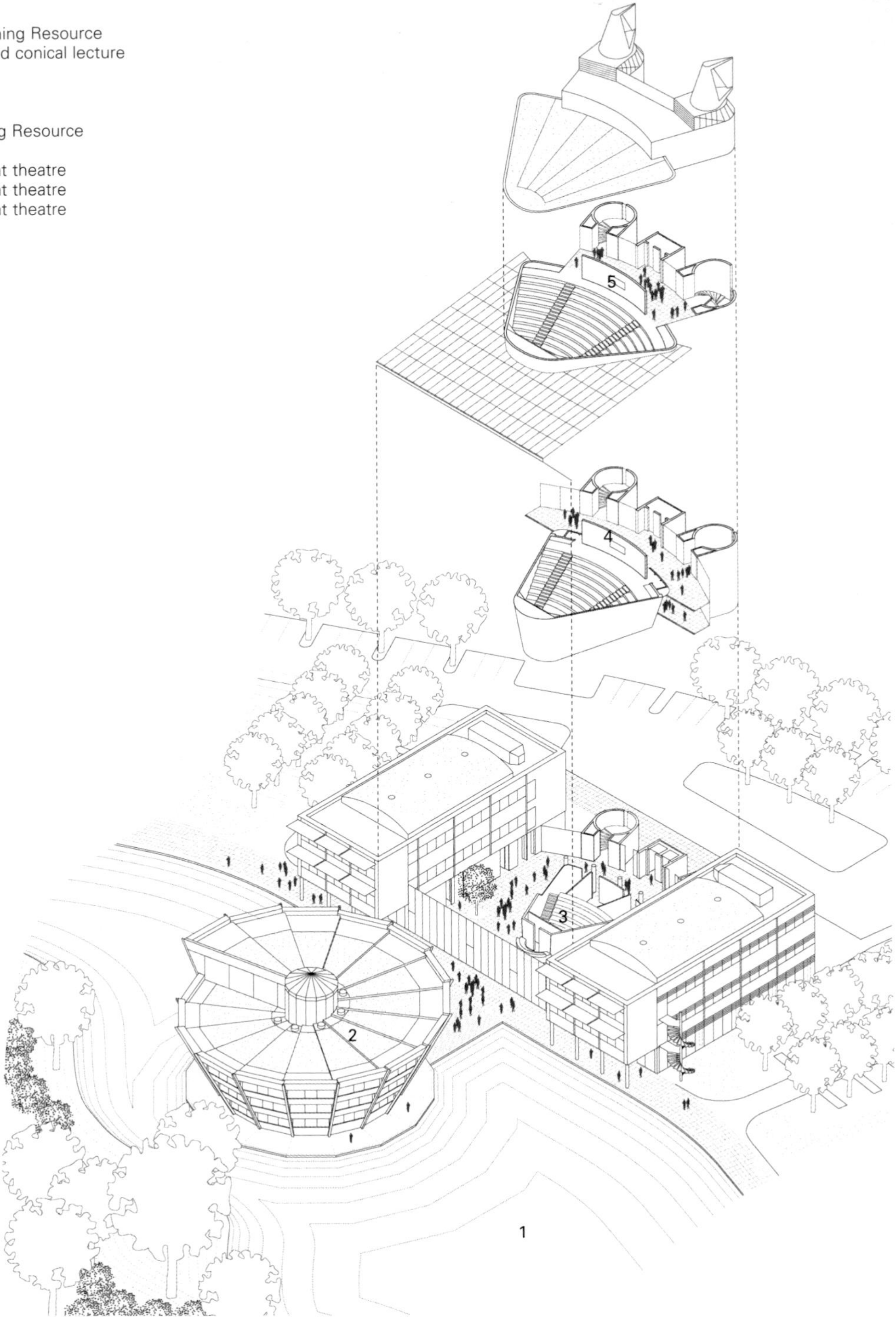

5

4

3

2

1

The faculty buildings
fronting the lake

Opposite page
The atrium spaces become
the natural social heart

Following pages
The Learning Resource
Centre is a focal point in
the campus organisation

Section

1 faculty wings
2 glazed atria
3 air handling units
4 rotating air cowl
5 glazed plant room
6 glazed atria

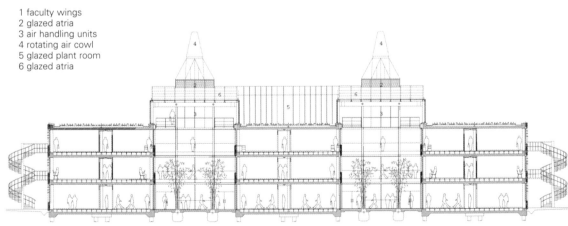

National College for School Leadership, University of Nottingham
2000–02

The National College for School Leadership is a building complex for conventions, seminars, and intensive continuing education courses for the teaching body.

This project concludes the site design of the Jubilee Campus with a radial structure directly overlooking a new artificial lake that completes the landscaping of the entire complex.

The urban scale, and the choices of space, materials and structures are in keeping with the rest of the campus, which thus takes on its own, distinct identity. Like the earlier structures, the new complex alternates three-storey buildings and glazed atriums of the same height. The structure was built on a web of beams and columns, and the exteriors have wood panelling with galvanised steel profiling. The atria are covered by garden roofs gently sloping down to the lake.

This compositional continuity, however, is contradicted by a few variants that set the new building apart. Hopkins abandoned the rectilinear layout of the earlier buildings to create an original curvilinear development along the lakeshore, redefining the relationships between building and nature with a single architectonic gesture.

The alternating rhythm of solidity (blocks) and transparency (atria) is further developed by the insertion of two single-storey volumes for the auditorium and the dining room. These two edifices with their wedge-shaped plans create the axis for the radial distribution of the straight blocks. The alternation of solid and transparent areas and the composition of the volumes creates a dynamic profile from both frontal and cross-section perspectives.

The classrooms and spaces for socialising are all concentrated on the ground floor: the atrium is used for eating and relaxation, and is animated by the lake views. The first and second floors. Are given over entirely to hotel-style bedrooms with en-suite bathrooms.

The atria, which are designed with passive cooling, are flexible spaces that may be reorganised using lightweight partitions to fit different needs: at the centre, a powerful circular staircase leads to the upper floors where guest rooms are located.

A sculptural object occupies the central atrium: this egg-shaped structure hovering on the axis of the main entry at the first floor level is really a free-access computer room, and is intended to symbolise the value of computers and virtual realty, the basis of all contemporary communication.

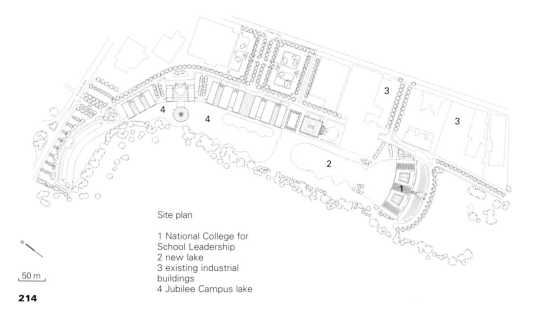

Site plan

1 National College for School Leadership
2 new lake
3 existing industrial buildings
4 Jubilee Campus lake

50 m

Exploded isometric of
central meeting space

Opposite page
A view across meeting
space

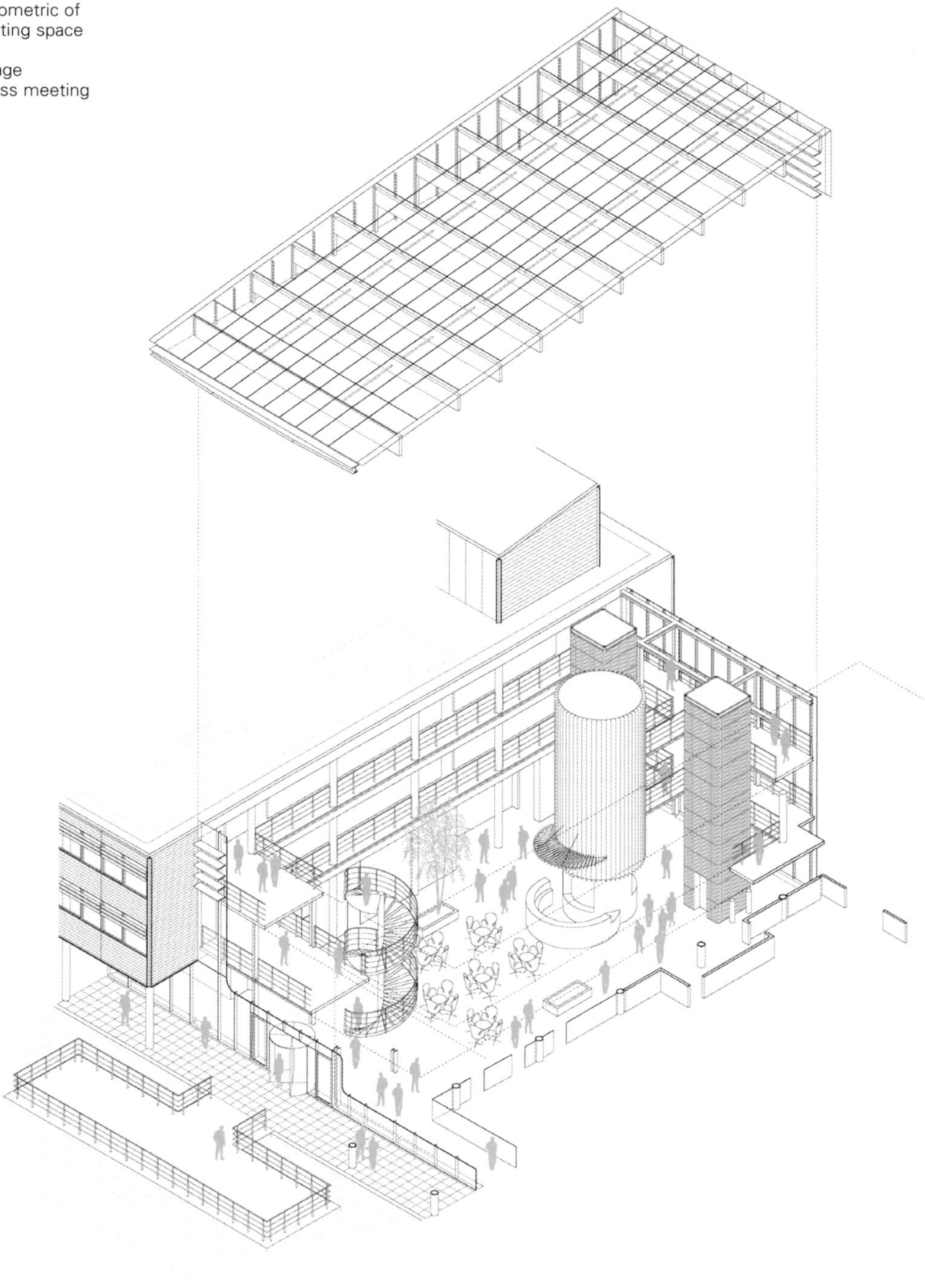

The Pilkington Laboratories, Sherborne School
Dorset
1995–2000

hool complex is located in a series of 19th- and 20th-century buildings in a cluster north of the Medieval Abbey Church of St Mary, in the historic centre of the small town of Sherborne, in the heart of the Dorset countryside.

The original intention was to reorganise the school's campus the better to integrate the buildings and make them more functional. Hopkins, an old boy of the school, proposed a plan that included the refurbishing of the Carrington Building, the demolition of a block of five courts, and the building of a new academic complex with a circular lecture theatre.

However, funds and financing from the Arts Council and Sports Council were not forthcoming and only a fraction of the target sum was raised. Thus the project had to be downsized, ambitions curtailed, and in the end, a single new building was built, to house the physics, chemistry and electronics laboratories. Hopkins designed a rectangular, two-storey block. Despite the domestic scale of the new building, there were no attempts to prettify the exterior, which remains elegant and light, in keeping with the medieval character of local architecture. The choice of sobriety was particular-

ly appropriate even because the main façade along Acreman Street frontage needed to fit into a sensitive urban setting consisting of a series of cottages and a handsome, two-storey residence.

The block consists of two units connected by a central corridor, the roofing reflects the organisation of the floor plan and central roof lights above the corridor connect two double-pitched roofs. Along the ridge four chimneys break up the overall horizontal rhythm of the composition. The geometric starkness is emphasised by external walls of load-bearing white brickwork faced with local Ham stone, in keeping with neighbouring buildings. The façade is characterised by two bands of regular, repetitive four-light windows set in the walls with reconstructed stone mullions. The rear façade is divided in the same manner, except that a colonnade replaces the windows on the first floor, and is separated from the chemistry laboratories inside by panels covered with wood.

The entrances are positioned along the short sides: the nearly storey-height difference in ground level made it possible to eliminate any internal vertical organisation as this is resolved by two external flights of stairs.

An open colonnade leading to the classrooms has a collegiate feel

The laboratories haul
a timeless quality within
the town

Opposite page
Entry to the colonnade

First floor plan

1 chemistry laboratories
2 preparation room
3 office
4 store
5 colonnade

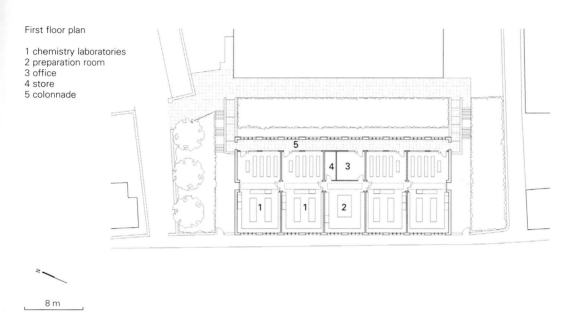

8 m

Cross section

1 chemistry laboratories
2 colonnade
3 corridor
4 physics laboratory

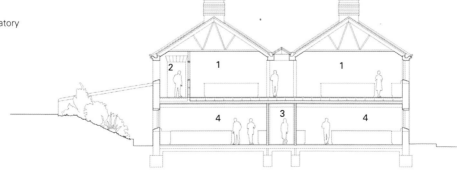

3 m

Education
The National Tennis Centre
Roehampton, London, SW15
1999–2007

This project was to develop a National Tennis Centre: similar centres have already been built in France, Belgium, Spain, Switzerland, Italy and America and have greatly benefited this sport's popularity.

The search for a site with the right national and international connections was long and complex, but ended when an area owned by the Bank of England southwest of London became available. The 17-hectare site was in Roehampton, between Barnes and Richmond Park, mostly surrounded by a wall making the area extremely private, and was already home to a golf course and other sports facilities for the express use of bank employees.

The new complex involves the creation of six covered courts, eight open-air courts, accommodations, offices, a medical centre, and conference halls.

The project aims to integrate the architecture perfectly into its natural setting. Thus, to minimise the environmental impact, the project is developed around the lie of the land: terracing with a 5-meter difference in level suggested the placement of the main entrance on the first floor level along Priory Lane. The imposing volume of the indoor courts is attenuated by the presence of volumes with elevations lower than those of the residence halls and service buildings, breaking up the volume into elements more in keeping with the human and urban scale of the context.

The planimetric organisation is divided into three main blocks: sports facilities, the reception, and administrative offices.

The reception occupies an entirely glazed structure that is identifiable by its fibreglass membrane structure and forms the axis around which the gymnasiums and offices revolve. The transparency of the glass offers views onto tennis courts immersed in Nature. This strategic use of materials involves the visitor directly and immediately.

The first floor entry leads directly to the balcony overlooking the indoor tennis courts: in addition to offering the space an obvious advantage on a psychological level, this raised access simplifies circulation. The walkway balcony leads, on the right, to offices and the sports injury clinic; on the left, to facilities and dormitories (16 double rooms, 4 single rooms for people with disabilities, and an apartment with two double rooms), organised in groups of four rooms alternating with a balcony or stairwell set back with respect to the line of the facade.

To the right of the reception may be found the offices and administrative building: a volume with a central atrium and circular stairway around which two floors of freeform offices flow.

The skyline is defined by the minimum of 9 m over the nets on the tennis courts: this requirement generated the roof design with pre-oxidized green copper panel cladding. to fit in with the surrounding landscape. There are a pair of arches on either side of each court connected to gently sloping pitched roofs on the perimeter blocks. The building is essentially a framed structure: an exposed concrete post and beam system based on the basic dimensions of a tennis court module required by the dimensions of the tennis courts, with a 36.6 meter clear span at the centre.

The first floor juts out 1.8 m. In addition to sheltering the ground floor, this overhang constitutes the foundation of the ring of walkways linking the different buildings. A painted steel structure supporting the deep overhang of the eaves is anchored to the first- storey floor slab; louvred shutters complete the sun protection on the first floor.

The priority of making the facility fit in harmoniously with the natural setting influenced many of the project decisions, among them the conscious effort to break up the building mass into smaller components, crowning them with the delicate design of the copper roofing. The dialogue with the exterior is emphasized by the presence of natural materials that strengthen the relationship between Nature and Sport.

Opposite page
Site plan

1 entrance
2 reception
3 courtyard
4 office
5 void over covered tennis courts
6 gymnasium
7 rehabilitation
8 medical centre
9 bedrooms

A model view of the
scope of the development

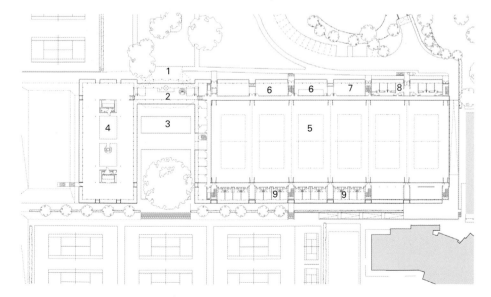

The New Science Building, Bryanston School

Blandford, Dorset

2002–07

In the autumn of 2002 Hopkins won the limited competition to design the new building for the Bryanston School Science Faculty. The brief required a project that was sensitive to the context and able to relate the new edifice to the existing complex, while taking into account future improvements. The architecture was thus designed with a flexible structural system that would be able to integrate future expansions and, at the same time, fit in with its surroundings and the established buildings.

The project proposes a building of three-floors with a semi-circular courtyard to accommodate the Biology, Physics, Chemistry and Maths departments, in addition to a 160sq.m. auditorium for conferences and seminars.

The shape of the new architecture is determined by the desire to integrate a variety of spaces and to create a continuity with Norman Shaw's original architecture, as well as with the more recent building by Piers Gough. Classrooms are arranged around the courtyard like fingers projecting from the main body of the building. This organisation stresses the relationship with the landscape, making the most of the view, with the added benefit of natural daylight and ventilation.

The new addition to the school complex contributes to the regeneration of links between the existing buildings, thanks to its unity of design.

First floor plan

1 lecture theatre
2 mathematics classroom
3 chemistry laboratory
4 chemistry prep room
5 assignment space
6 science garden
7 greenhouse

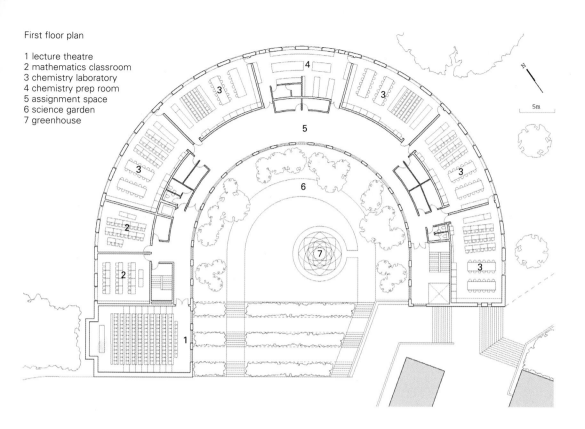

Cross section

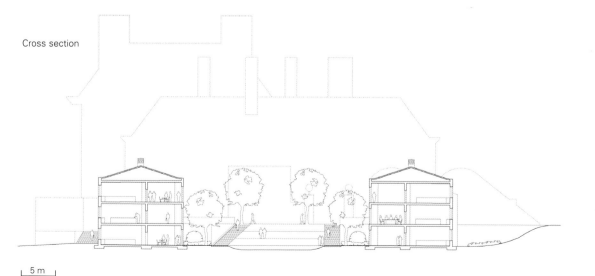

5 m

Northern Arizona University Advanced Research and Development Facility
Flagstaff, Arizona, USA
2003–

The building brings ecological and biological research departments together with local, innovative small business's to create a new hybrid type of University building. The brief calls for a LEED platinum building and aims to become the greenest building in the United States!

The building has a curved form with a full-height atrium orientated to optimise for passive solar collection. This heats the building completely by the power of the sun in the winter and during the summer, a simple yet a technologically advanced, passive ventilation and cooling strategy will be employed to keep the building comfortable. Local materials such as Navajo Sandstone and Ponderosa Pine will be used on the façades to create a contextual and suitable response to the local climate and culture. All these building systems will be integrated into the building fabric in a way that allows students to learn by observing. The building, in this sense, becomes a pedagogical, living laboratory.

Sectional model showing
the distribution of spaces

Education
The Kroon Building, School of Forestry and Environmental Studies Yale University
New Haven, USA
2005–

The Kroon Building is a new faculty building for the School of Forestry at Yale University in the United States. The site of the Kroon building is located on the western side of "Science Hill", the centre of the University's scientific community.

The School of Forestry's brief to Hopkins Architect's was to introduce a building which would act as a cohesive element and focus for their 'micro' campus, unifying the currently dispersed and separate faculty buildings across Science Hill, and addressing the needs of a growing department.

The structure accommodates offices for the faculty, classrooms and teaching spaces, a library and study center. The focus of the building is the double height oak paneled third floor which contains an auditorium for 175 people and the "The Environment Center', a flexible space which will host exhibitions and symposia.

The building should aim to establish a strong sense of architectural identity for the School of Forestry, which would also demonstrate the University's wider commitment to sustainable design. In addition the building should also accommodate all the functions, which would make it the social and academic focus for the study of issues of sustainability.

Hopkin's responded by placing a simple rectangular form between the neo gothic Osbourn Memorial Laboratory and Sage Bowers Hall, mediating and sub dividing the space between them to create two new courtyards, which are the focus of social activities and ceremonies at Yale, and at the same time reintroducing the Yale collegiate urban structure to this area of Science Hill.

One side of the building is buried into the sloping site, allowing access to the north on the first floor and the south on the ground floor, as well as making new connections between the existing buildings, knitting together the separate buildings of the faculty. The whole building is also placed on a raised podium, which addresses the imbalance of the imposing gothic façade of the OML building to the south by bringing the new building up to an equal level and scale.

The west elevation of the building boldly 'announces' the presence of the faculty on Prospect Street, and through its transparent glass elevation allows views into the workings of the building. In contrast the west elevation opens out onto the green open space and trees of historic Sachem's Wood.

In both its siting and form the Kroon Building aims to response to and enhance its context. The building is a 4 storey rectangular volume with a steep pitched roof, echoing the context of the form of traditional Yale neo gothic colleges. It is constructed from a combination of contextual natural and contemporary materials; stone, concrete, steel and glass.

The north and south walls are constructed from coursed local sandstone with precast concrete window surrounds, lintols and quoins. The east and west walls are fully glazed with solid timber external louvers to limit solar gain but also to retain daylight and views into the building. The south side of the roof is covered with an array of photovoltaic panels. The interiors of the building are lined with oak paneling from Yale's own forests.

The building is due to be completed in 2008.

View of the building
in its context

Model of the campus

Chemistry Building, Princeton University
New Jersey, USA
2005–

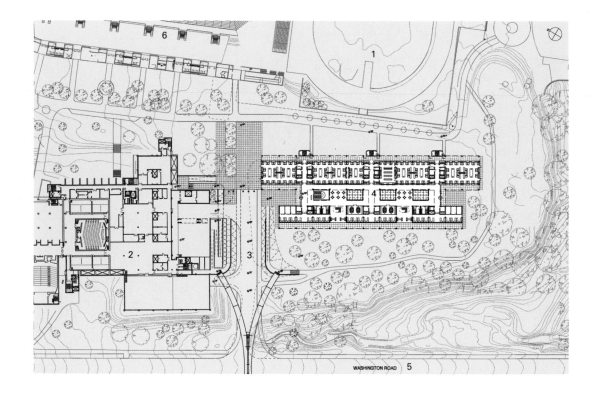

The project is for a low-energy use research laboratory and teaching facility that will meet the highest technical specifications, while providing an attractive working environment.

The new Chemistry Building is designed to integrate general teaching and high-level research, and planned to enhance collaboration and creativity. All communicating spaces are designed to promote formal and casual interaction.

The building massing expresses its programmatic organisation; the faculty offices are accommodated in

the towers facing the Campus woodland, whilst teaching and research laboratories are housed in a deep linear block to the rear. Circulation between these two spaces is via a central glazed atrium. This structure filters natural light into laboratory and conference spaces, becoming the main place of assembly.

The building is located on a "gateway" site, at a promontory over one of the principle entrances to the University Campus. It is a new component of a wider planning effort aiming to consolidate a 'science neighbourhood' that would involve all of Princeton's science buildings.

Opposite page
Site plan

1 Princeton University
stadium
2 Jadwin hall
3 Armory Lane
4 New chemistry building
5 Washington Road
6 Palmer Stadium

Bottom
Visualisation of the project

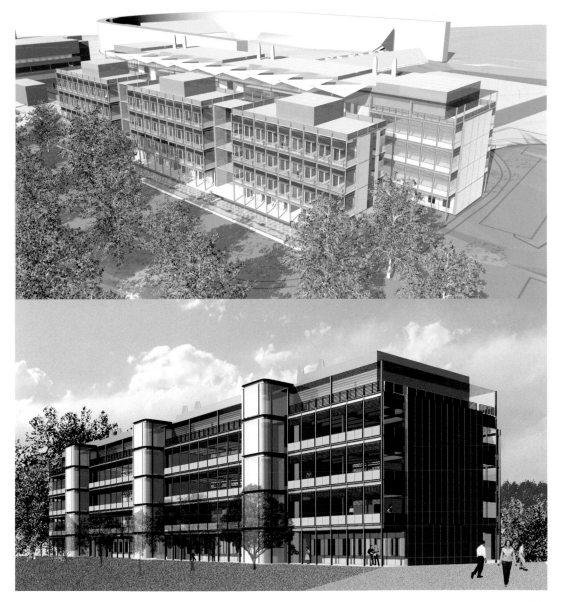

Queen's Building,
Emmanuel College
Cambridge
1993–95

This project presents analogies with the Glyndebourne Opera House where *memory* and *context* are sources of innovation. The assignment comes from the English Establishment which, while accepting *modernity* – as long as it is branded "Hopkins"–, also measures it against the eternal value of the tradition of one of the oldest university institutions.

Hopkins proposed a rigorous single volume building, with a strong materiality: a freestanding building, where the colour and texture of the stone give a sculptural quality upon the composition.

The building is only visible in glimpses from Parker Street and, as tradition would have it, it is mostly accessible from the private and half-hidden streets of Emmanuel College, to which it belongs, both culturally and physically. Set in a context with a strong historic identity, the new architecture pays homage to Christopher Wren. It employs the same Ketton limestone that Wren used to build the college's baroque chapel, in a "homage", or perhaps taking up the "challenge" to update the language of an ancient material, by using original shapes and building procedures.

The new building, known as Queen's Building, houses a theatre and the college common rooms. The powerful, oval form is symmetrical along the longitudinal axis: on the first floor, a solid wall wraps around the building above the open colonnade on the ground floor and the wide windows on the second floor.

The austere main entry is located at the centre of the plan where a passageway cuts through the ground floor, crossing its longitudinal axis. Two circular stairs provide vertical distribution: the first is inside and near the entry, while the second is outside in a tower of glass blocks that is almost freestanding. It is linked to the building by a frameless glazed path, a sort of emblematically transparent umbilical cord that unites, separates and "nourishes" modernity and tradition. The apsidal rooms on the ground and first floors contain the senior and junior common rooms music practice rooms. On the first and second floor a theatre seats one hundred and seventy: an austere space with two stairs that frame the tiered seating and lead to a gallery lit by a strip of modular openings.

Sobriety and clarity pervade the aesthetic of the interior and exterior where the number of materials is limited: stone for the walled areas, stainless steel for the tension rods and nuts, light American oak for the panelling of the interiors.

The lead-clad shallow-pitched roof is barely perceptible from the outside. Meanwhile, the wraparound façade in stone confers an essential aspect that, upon more careful analysis, reveals itself in all its innovative structural complexity: a network of reinforced stone pillars connected by stone lintols that create a grid, in-filled with pre-fabricated, non-load bearing stone panels. The load bearing structure is distinguishable from the stone facing by a thin groove running along the perimeters of the panels, which are also differentiated from the pillars by their size.

Hopkins' philosophy, which banks on structural honesty, requires the stone masonry to be load bearing, but the limited thickness of the pillars (40 cm) is insufficient for resisting the thrust of the floors and roof. Thus, tensioned stainless steel rods are inserted through stainless steel tubes at the centre of the pre-cast, concrete kneeling blocks. This reinforcement of the stone is a modern-day version of the medieval technology of buttress and pinnacles.

The curve of the flat arches creates a moment of torsion that is contrasted by the containing action of the eaves and the concrete floor, which are anchored to the pillars by a fair-face concrete padstone.

The display of the materials in their essential beauty is fundamental to communicating a project that is coherent from the inside to the outside and that is treated with a building philosophy whose origins go back to Pugin.

As an expression of Hopkins' mature style, the Queen's Building refines the elements he used in previous projects: the roof covering reminds us of the David Mellor factory, the glass block tower of those used at the Inland Revenue Centre in Nottingham, the planimetric layout and building logic of those seen at Glyndebourne Opera House. This architecture does not aim to flaunt originality, but to show innovation as a result of patient and constant research.

Site plan

1 Queen's Building
2 Front Court
3 The Wren Chapel
4 Master's Lodge
5 The Old Library

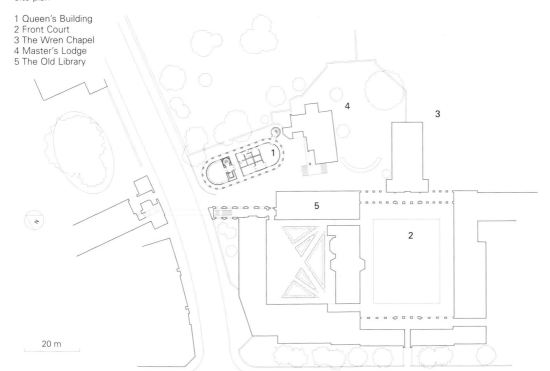

20 m

A view from the Fellows garden

Opposite page
A new route for the College through the Queen's building

Longitudinal section

1 reception room
2 Middle Common Room
3 junior common reading room
4 auditorium
5 foyer

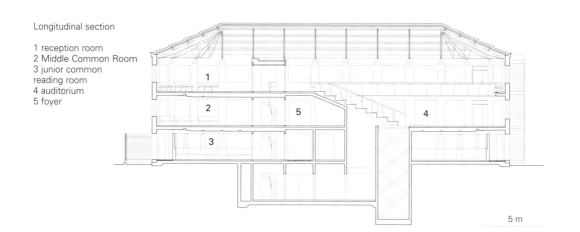

5 m

First floor plan

1 Middle Common Room
2 foyer
3 auditorium

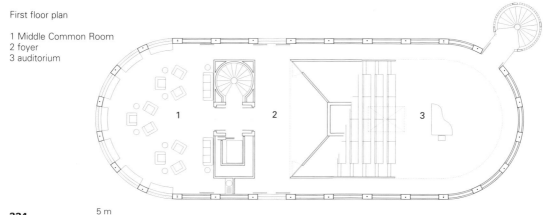

5 m

Lady Sarah Cohen House
London, N11
1993–96

This care home for one hundred and twenty elderly and disabled residents rises up in a verdant park on the outskirts of a residential neighbourhood in north London. The area is configured as a green lung, a haven of peace within the oppression of the city, but one that nonetheless takes advantage of the availability of services and infrastructures. The building stands at the end of a driveway separates residents from the noise of the busy streets along the southern side of the lot. It is positioned off centre to the left of the site in order to make the most of the extension of the park and its old oak and willow trees. This park is the result of an intense landscaping campaign that began with assigning a position of honour to the oldest oak, at the centre of the roundabout at the end of the driveway, right before the care home entrance.

After years researching elegant corporative aesthetics, this project offers an opportunity to try out different skills, such as sensitively reinventing the care-home, transforming anonymous spaces into spaces for socializing and for privacy, within an intimate and domestic atmosphere. As Michael Hopkins points out, the scheme grows out of the idea of redefining the care-home as "a place for a stay in the country", and the patients as "guests" or "residents". English care design in the Nineties had not yet studied the requalification of the standards that were successively introduced by the privatization processes in the sector. Thus, the challenge was to formulate a schematic approach able to harmonize sometimes-conflicting priorities such as the need for autonomy and privacy, as well as security and socialization in a home that succeeds in communicating a sense of belonging.

Hopkins proposes an architecture that is elegantly minimalist. In fact, there are no formal concessions or aesthetic virtuosities, but "authentic" choices for the project, resulting in a building with a clear constructive logic, formal and functional.

The four-floored square building develops around a courtyard: the ground floor accommodates shared activities; the next three have groups of accommodations of forty rooms per floor, as well as dining rooms, living rooms and consultation rooms. Thus, each floor forms a little autonomous "neighbourhood" that helps individualize the impersonality of the institutional hospital block.

The project offers a typological hierarchy of interfaced public and private spaces ranging from the court, the public space par excellence, to the bay windows with seats for private reading, conversation with a family member, or meditation in front of the panorama of the park and city.

The ground floor, where the cafes, swimming pools and common areas are located, looks onto the courtyard that is enriched with flowerbeds and places to stop, and may be accessed through doors along a glazed cloister. Room layouts make use of circulation along a single distribution corridor that is symmetrical with respect to the depth of the building and opens at the corners with bays for resting with windowseats. These bays are also used for wheel chair manoeuvring.

The most difficult task was to humanize the hospital institution and succeed in integrating safety requirements within the design: one such example is the substitution of the guide for wheelchairs with a resistant light oak covering that is easy to maintain.

Materials are always given natural expression: plain wood, glass, brick, steel, are shown to their best advantage, as we are now accustomed to enjoy them in a consolidated tradition of projects, from the Glyndebourne Opera to the Auditorium at Emmanuel College at Cambridge, where the colours and textures of the materials exalt interiors and exteriors with analogous treatments.

This care home is an emblematic example of two worlds that are coming closer to one another: tradition and modernity. The brick structure, the court scheme, the cloister and the traditional English bay windows are treated with the purism and building ethic that is typical of mature High–Tech.

Ground floor plan

1 reception
2 waiting
3 café
4 synagogue
5 library
6 office
7 doctor
8 kitchen
9 laundry
10 hydrotherapy
11 physiotherapy
12 recreational therapy
13 hairdresser
14 courtyard

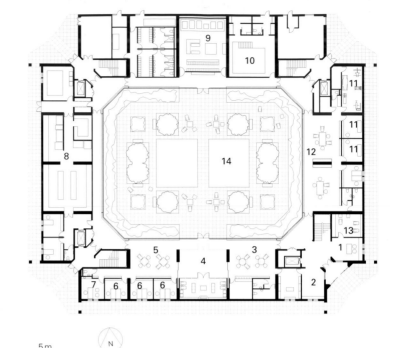

5 m

N

First floor plan

1 dining area
2 sitting area
3 sister's office
4 treatment room
5 assisted bathroom

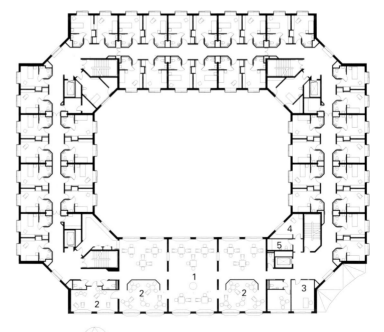

5 m

N

External view

A view into the central
courtyard

Collegiate
Sheltered Housing, Charterhouse
London, EC1
1994–2000

Charterhouse is a building complex in the City of London that takes its name from the Carthusian priory on the site from 1371 until the 1530s, when Henry VIII ordered the dissolution of the monasteries.

An aristocratic mansion was built where the priory once stood and was later transformed into an almshouse and school. In 1872, the school was moved to Surrey, while the almshouse, known as Sutton Hospital, was converted into a home for elderly men and continues to serve this purpose today.

The complex consists of a collection of different buildings from various dates spanning five hundred years around a system of collegiate-style courts.

Built in 1820 and heavily bombed during the Second World War, the Preacher's Court fell into a state of abandon, and the south-west perimeter of the court in particular needed to be rebuilt. Shielded by a tall wall along St Johns Street, the project consists of two free-standing buildings that redefine the confines of the courtyard. The first is a block with a square plan with two flats on the first floor and a small library on the ground floor; the second, with a rectangular plan on three floors, houses twelve flats arranged around two lift and staircase cores.

Very simple and rational, the two buildings are arranged at right angles to one another, and have similar formal and building characteristics: masonry walls a brick and a half thick, and flat arches to define the window openings and modular porticoes on the ground floor; parapets with stone coping cover the eaves and hide the shallow-pitched, lead-clad roofs.

The façades are rigorously arranged with frameless openings alternating windows and cast aluminium bays. The outer walls on the ground floor are clad in oak panels, a solution used in previous projects such as the Queen's Building at Emmanuel College and the Pilkington Laboratories for the Sherbourne School.

The flats are distributed in order to maximize the space that is lit by the ample windows overlooking the courtyard. The rooms and salons are panelled with wood stained a light magnolia; bathrooms and kitchens are equipped with luxury fittings. The stairwells have roof lights and are treated like outdoor spaces with fair-faced brick walls.

The library stairwell is open, like those at the colleges at Oxford and Cambridge.

As is usual in Hopkins' work, this project fits into a landscape of green spaces and pavements made of York stone.

The materials express nature's potential with analogous treatments for interiors and exteriors: wood, glass, brickwork, steel, are all enhanced by juxtapositions that exalt the natural material qualities of colours and textures.

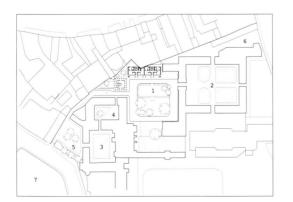

Site plan

1 Preacher's Court
2 Pensioners Court
3 Masters Court
4 Wash-house Court
5 entrance court
6 Stable court
7 Charterhouse Square

Interior view of a flat

Entrance off the covered colonnade

Opposite page
View of landscaped courtyard

Collegiate
Haberdashers' Hall
London, EC1
1996–2002

Founded in 1448 by Henry VI, the Worshipful Company of Haberdashers is one of the "Great Twelve" livery companies of the City of London.

Since the fifteenth century, the Company has had headquarters in three different locations: Hopkins designed the fourth, near Smithfield market, within a "backyard" site that was already built around its roadside perimeters. The project is conceived as an urban enclave only fragmentary glimpses of which may be caught through an opening along Bridge Street. The plan's objective is to generate new boundaries within which a small urban oasis may be built. The immediate typological reference is the Oxford College with the porter's lodge and quad that, in this case, translates as a block with a central court and a two-floored cloistered building with reception rooms as well as offices and flats.

The new headquarters thus has no public façades. It is a self-contained construction, revolving around a perfectly square private court, closed on three sides by continuous façades in brickwork marked out by a modular arrangement of arches and flat arches quoting the structure of the Glyndebourne Opera.

The main entrance, at the centre of an imposing Edwardian warehouse, opens onto a hall that leads to a large loggia, an atrium and finally a majestic stairway. The vanishing spaces that are at first public and become increasingly hidden and private transform the entrance into an experience of classical spatial effects where axiality and symmetry presage the magnificence of the interiors. North of the entry, the loggia ends in an atrium offering two different itineraries: the one to the left leads to the Orangery, a glazed fair-faced brickwork portico; the one to the right leads to a theatrical spiral stair within a brick drum with rooflight illumination.

On the first floor, a long foyer (5 m x 30 m) constitutes the social space shared by three main rooms: at centre is the Courtroom, an apsidial auditorium, symmetrically flanked by the banquet room and meeting room. At the end of the foyer is a small, square atrium leading to the west wing, which is entirely dedicated to the grand Livery Hall, where receptions, conferences and formal dinners are held.

Unlike other rooms, which have plastered concrete ceilings, the Livery Hall (10 x 20 m) has a ceiling of laminated timber beams on a diagonal grid in-filled by white oak panels, which also clad the walls. The result is an uninterrupted smooth, enveloping space. A network of laminated timber beams held together by cross-shaped stainless steel shoes supports the structure of the ceiling, which is on a 45° angle. Each diamond shape consists of four beams and four panels fitted together to confer a smooth aspect upon the surface. Steel tie-rods form a web supporting the ceiling and are anchored in a series of pre-fabricated concrete corbels resting on load bearing brick pillars.

This innovative system is a modern version of medieval building techniques, in particular the truss system, transformed into a three-dimensional web of laminated tie beams and tie rods.

The design of the lead-clad roof reflects the structural gridwork of the wood panelled interior.

The same design approach is applied to both the interior and exterior, emphasizing the performance and texture of materials: the different components (wood panels, brick flat arches, concrete slabs) are always readable thanks to the clear design lines stressing the separate nature of their hierarchy.

The building thus appears as if it were sculpted out of the material: constructive minimalism and honesty guide the project, making no concessions to established practices even when ancient materials such as wood and brick are used. The loadbearing structure determines the shape and style of the building: two orders of tapered pillars and flat arches define a portico on the ground floor where wide glazed openings enhance the dematerialization of the wall. The elegant continuity of the texture of the brickwork is also due to the use of lime mortar, which eliminates any need for expansion joints.

The typological references to university buildings at Oxford and cultural references to classical architecture are merely the involuntary result of research driven by interests grounded in an all-new philosophy: proportion and symmetry are the expressive means for the parts of a whole, to be assembled with uncompromising rigour, but with strength for a new concept of tectonic display.

First floor plan

1 Livery Hall
2 reception gallery
3 luncheon room
4 court room
5 committee room
6 main stair
7 display room
8 drawing room
9 library
10 Master's flat
11 Beadle's flat
12 Clerk's flat

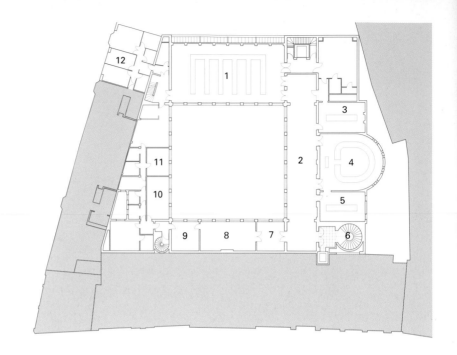

Ground floor plan

1 entrance hall
2 porter's lodge
3 loggia
4 courtyard
5 colonnade
6 orangery
7 cloaks
8 offices
9 kitchen
10 loading bay
11 service yard

Opposite page
The hall surrounds a
landscaped courtyard

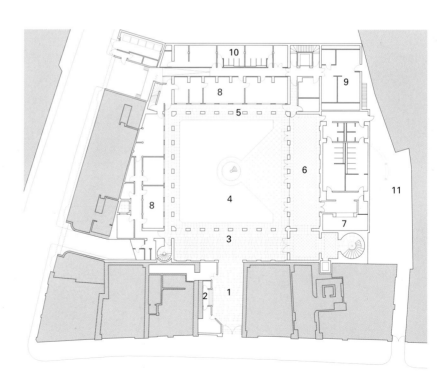

248

Health Care
Evelina Children's Hospital
London, SE1
1999–2005

The new Evelina Children's Hospital is part of the hospital division of Guys and St Thomas, one of the capital's primary hospitals. Throughout a period lasting over a hundred years, the St Thomas' hospital site has grown with new constructions attesting to the evolution of hospital planning. It is an historic document expressing the theories of Henry Curry and Florence Nightingale, in the "French pavilions" inaugurated in 1871 by Queen Victoria, and those of Eugene Rosenberg, who in the 1970s adopted the American organization, with centralized services surrounded by a wide ward.

Evelina, a structure offering 140 beds (20 of which are for intensive therapy), represents Hopkins' first large-scale hospital project. The brief required a solution that would represent the latest practice of this complex building type. It referred to the most recent psychological research regarding space and had the following goals:
– to take advantage of the vicinity of Archibishop's Park, with vistas onto the green lung of Lambeth and glimpses of London,
– to emphasize the relationship with the city, placing the principal entry along Lambeth Palace Road,
– to regenerate the entire medical area, creating the basis for developing a second artery along New Lambeth Road to link the new Children's Hospital and St Thomas'.

The structure consists of a 7-storey building characterized by the powerful glass curtain of the conservatory resting on a three-storey podium. From the third floor, the façade rises to the roof with the curved profile of the conservatory, and that has a steel diagrid structure to which glass panels and projecting sunshades are anchored.

This technological virtuosity allows views over the park to create an inside-outside dialogue between the hospital-city and the metropolitan city with obvious psychotherapeutic benefits. The podium of the building thus joins the taller part by means of this connecting element, which gives the hospital its morphology and identity.

The conservatory (65 x 15 x 20 m tall), becomes the centre of gravity, the fulcrum of the hospital's interactive life: a space of utmost flexibility that can fulfil the role of playroom, school, meeting area, exhibition and performance space,, and café for the hospital community.

Thus the space within the conservatory refreshes the entire concept of hospitalization, generating new criteria for space distribution, following the logic placing public services on the lower floors, and functions that require more tranquillity, such as inpatient accommodation and specialised departments, on upper floors. storage and parking are at basement level; reception, public facilities and outpatient consulting rooms are on the ground floor; on the first floor are the day hospital, the academic areas, and imaging department; on the second floor are the operating theatres and intensive care unit; on the third floor, specialised departments (urology and dialysis); on the fourth and fifth floors are rooms for inpatients; on the sixth floor, health administration.

It has two entries: a public one, opening onto the city, along Lambeth Road, and an internal one that offers access to St Thomas' Hospital.

The two entryways are located at the ends of a longitudinal concourse along which the general distribution of the building takes place. Symbolizing a city street, it is designed to ease orientation. It is punctuated by two scarlet structures that transform the vertical distribution towers into beacons for easy wayfinding. Within these structures are the glazed cabins of the "wall climber rocket" lifts that shoot skyward, while offering a view of the hospital's entire internal life.

Horizontal distribution follows a central axis that is repeated on each floor and offers views of the service stair and different functional areas.

No more tight narrow spaces, but open, flexible ones characterize the project's innovation. The 18-metre inpatient wards are divided longitudinally into three areas: single rooms to the north, inpatient areas overlook the conservatory side, services and staff rooms in the centre. Circulation is left free and fluid.

From the construction point of view, a structural grid was adopted measuring 9 x 7.2 m based on the classic model of a ward. Raised floors were avoided for reasons of hygiene, and cables were housed in the suspended ceilings. Interiors were designed to make the experience as pleasurable as possible for young patients. Particular care was taken with regard to materials and colours, which were chosen in collaboration with children. Light and transparency are always favoured in order to create exterior visual contact. This develops a new idea for hospital buildings that are no longer inward looking, but seek the maximum integration with the urban context it belongs to.

Shapes and colours are used to identify the different levels using the natural world: the ocean, the arc-

tic, the forest, the beach, the savannah, the mountains and the sky. These are developed by comprehensible images that lighten the environment and stimulate the imagination of the young patients.

This innovative hospital is efficient, human, and with a high architectonic value. The glass and steel conservatory is an original element that blends well with the terracotta rainscreen panels, that successfully turns a complex typology into an exercise in lightness and transparency.

A view from Lambeth
Palace Gardens

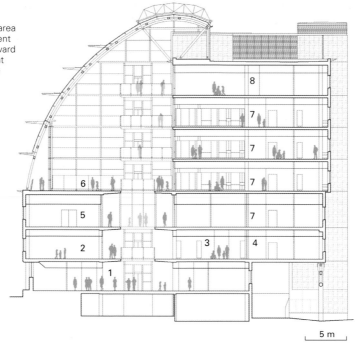

Cross section

1 outpatient waiting area
2 academic department
3 medical day case ward
4 imaging department
5 paediatric intensive
care unit
6 conservatory
7 ward
8 academic offices

5 m

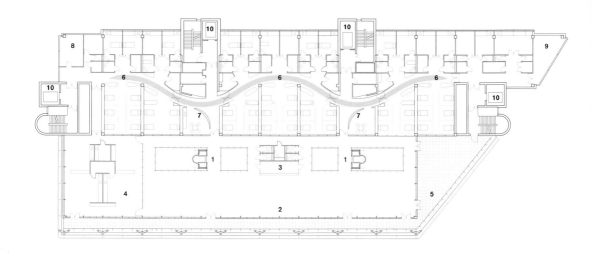

Third floor plan

1 "rocket lift"
2 conservatory
3 servery/café
4 school

5 terrace
6 inpatients
7 reception/play area
8 seminar
9 parents
10 bed lift and stair core

N

10 m

View towards the entrance
reception and the
outpatients waiting area

A patient's bed overlooking
the conservatory

Opposite page
A helter skelter to amuse
waiting children at
outpatients

The conservatory known
as "The Beach"

Health Care
Ambulatory Cancer Care Centre, University College London Hospitals
Tottenham Court Rd, London, W1
2005–

The new Ambulatory Cancer Care Centre will represent one of the first bio-medical campuses built in England to research guidelines developed in the United States.

The site is located in central London near the stations of Euston, St Pancras and King's Cross and then underground connections. It is also within walking distance of the city's main hospital and university buildings, thus offering it an excellent base for Clinical Research.

The site, known as "The Odeon Site" because it was once home to a well-known cinema, had been used as a car park since 1966, when the UCLH acquired it for that purpose and as a storage area. After considering various building schemes, the Foundation decided to redevelop the area, including an adjacent building, to create a modern Cancer Care Centre where patients may receive care and treatments in a day-hospital setting (bed provision is not planned), as well as an area dedicated to university research departments.

The project objective is to create a centre that makes the institutional hospital more human while offering flexibility and compatibility with its surroundings within the historic urban context.

Hopkins proposes a building developed around a central, internal atrium that will stretch the full height of the building; it will constitute the axis for vertical and horizontal circulation and act as the orientation space where the building's activities are made apparent to its users. The atrium is also the public space where socialisation takes place; it is the "heart" of the hospital's body and floods the entire complex with light. Its glazed panels allow a maximum amount of natural light and passive solar heat that may be controlled through external shading. Such attention to energy resources is coherent with the general policy of sustainable construction, which is a priority in contemporary innovation.

The external façade will include steel, glass, and stone, while the interior will be finished with fair-faced concrete, stone and glass. Materials will be harmoniously combined and treated with the expressive and structural honesty of an elegant structuralist matrix.

View of courtyard

Opposite page
View along the internal street

Chapter 4

The Sustainable City

Leon Battista Alberti stated that a city is like a large house.
The exploratory path, beginning with Hopkins House, led to the vision of the city of the future: a new city designed in accordance with the latest imperatives of innovative sustainability. Technology is no longer just a means to design high-performance objects but a powerful tool for tackling the architecture of the city.
The latest sustainable technologies have produced a language of construction that becomes form – that is, architecture according to the eternal Vitruvian triad of, *utilitas*, *firmitas* and *venustas* (commodity, firmness and delight). The circle closes, only to begin again…

Provincial Headquarter, Pisa, 2003

Provincial Headquarter
Pisa, Italy
2003
competition

In 2002 the Province of Pisa Authority held an international competition for the design of its new headquarters. The objective of Hopkins's scheme to affirm the new ideas of "sustainable town planning", linking the compositional choices not only to the technical themes of energy conservation but also to those, with broader cultural overtones, of environmental compatibility. The architecture is, therefore, the result of both the correct use of urban design and a commitment to create an identity of place that will last in time.

Thus, the scheme is generated from a careful analysis of the characteristics of the site and its relationship with the surrounding area. Cisanello and the spa town of San Giuliano Terme represent the historic urban models linked to the Italian tradition that identifies the piazza, the main street and monumental public building as the ingredients for the construction of the city: these are ancient elements that are to be found in the scale relationships and the organization of the vehicle and pedestrian routes and the volumes of the buildings in the scheme.

The new complex is, therefore, one of the first experiments with a sustainable city, in terms of both its insertion in the environment, taking into account the local culture, and its use of building techniques intended to favour the greatest possible energy conservation. This is made possible by typological solutions and materials that facilitate natural ventilation and, at the same time, allow lightness and transparency to assist the integration of the activities in the buildings.

The new buildings are concentrated along the edge of the site, forming a protective shell for the public area in the traffic-free centre; automobile circulation is channelled along the external ring road. The building types and the construction procedures are well-established ones: structures made of reinforced concrete cast *in situ*; fair-face brick cladding on both the exteriors and the interiors; wooden or aluminium door- and window-frames.

The distribution of functions respects the requirements set out in the competition guidelines: the public and commercial activities are concentrated on the ground floor; the north wing houses the directorate-general, the council chambers and the spatial planning department, while the productive activities are located in the south wing of the complex. A radial building enclosing the space on the west side has been designed for the library and other social and cultural functions. The environmental strategy is the principal objective of the planning, which follows tried-and-tested general techniques such as the climatic screen of trees and the external shading systems with internal filter areas. Energy conservation is of fundamental importance in the design choices, with a philosophy that could be summarized in the following basic criteria:
- buildings with a long-life cycle and durable materials;
- flexible spaces that can be adapted to different needs;
- use of local resources and products (ready for use where possible);

The San Giuliano Terme scheme showing the urban links and public spaces

Views of San Giuliano
Terme urban areas

- use of natural finishes such as fair-face concrete or wood;
- integrated elements with multiple effects, such as soffits in fair-face concrete with structural and environmental control functions and as an architectural finish;
- wherever possible, occupant-operated environmental controls, such as openable windows, sunshades, and perimeter heating;
- contact with the external environment – no occupant should be more than 8 m from natural light.

Energy consumption is reduced by the use of systems, such as the following:
- controlled glazed surfaces and external shading systems to reduce solar heat gain;
- maximization of thermal inertia to reduce rapid changes in temperature and minimize energy consumption;
- low pressure ventilation plant;
- underfloor distribution of air;
- use of groundwater for the cooling systems, rather than refrigeration units;
- recycling of grey water;
- low maintenance costs thanks to the robustness of the plant and efficient control systems.

Energy conservation and sustainability (use of photovoltaic panels for generating electricity, wind and solar energy for heating, ecological petrol substitutes, co-generation) are the key features on which the whole project is based, all achieved while maintaining a balance of urban scale and architectural integrity.

The strongly innovative concept of the project, which integrates architecture and emergent technologies, requires the financial support of third parties, such as the European Union, but evidently Italy is not yet ready to face the challenge of the future.

View of the model

1 Council meeting room
2 public area
3 parking
4 amphitheatre
5 meeting rooms
6 bar
7 public area
8 library

Bottom, left
The traditional architecture
of the main square
of San Giuliano Terme

Bottom, right, and opposite
page
Model views showing the
development within the
urban context: the green
area to be preserved during
the construction phases
and the completed scheme
with the existing trees

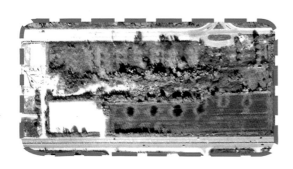

Section

1 courtyard
2 meeting areas
3 office areas
4 reception
5 Committee meeting room
6 Council meeting room

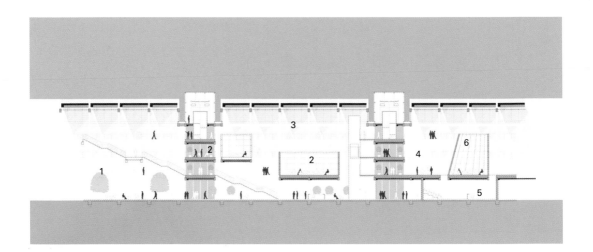

Plan

1 courtyard
2 office area
3 meeting areas
4 lift
5 Council meeting room

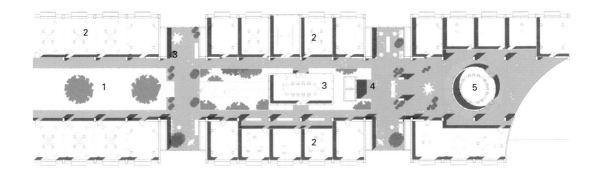

Section

1 roof overhang
2 prefabricated concrete slabs
3 brick cladding
4 services distribution floor
5 balcony
6 daylight is reflected from façade light shelves
7 internal walls are built with hallow local bricks
8 shaded walkway
9 traditional terracotta tiles
10 anodized aluminium louvres
11 glass louvres

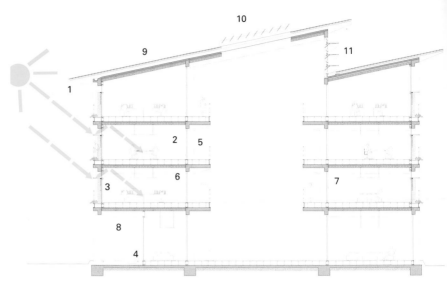

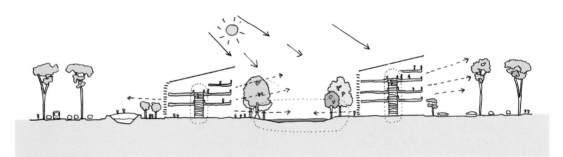

Diagram of the environmental and sustainable strategies

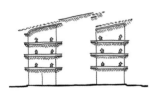

The pre-fabricated concrete structure assembled on site maximizes the thermal inertia reducing rapid changes in temperature

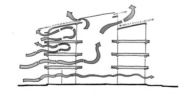

During the mid season natural ventilation is controlled by opening windows and light shelves; in summer a mechanical ventilation system is provided

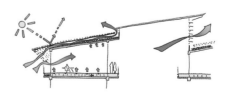

Natural ventilation provides cooling of the space in between the roof tiles and the concrete slab

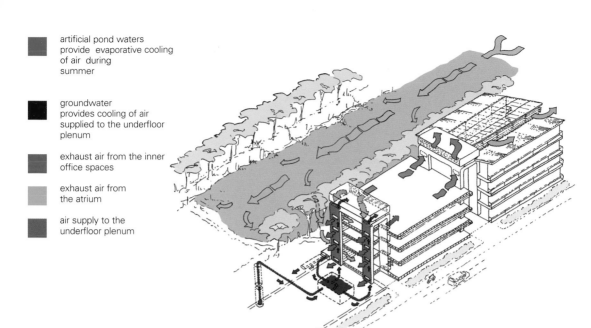

artificial pond waters
provide evaporative cooling
of air during
summer

groundwater
provides cooling of air
supplied to the underfloor
plenum

exhaust air from the inner
office spaces

exhaust air from
the atrium

air supply to the
underfloor plenum

Recreational areas
in the garden

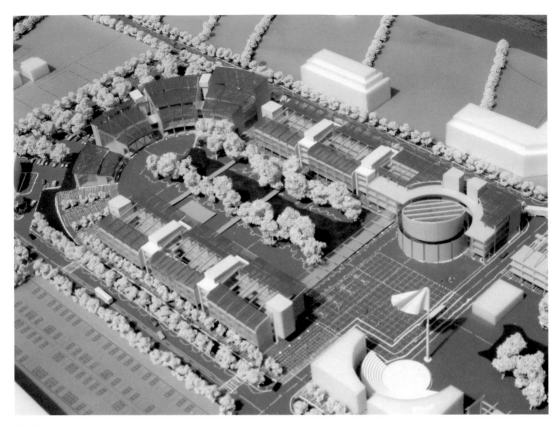

Model view

Construction phases

Exsisting site

Phase 1 - The new
Provincial headquarter

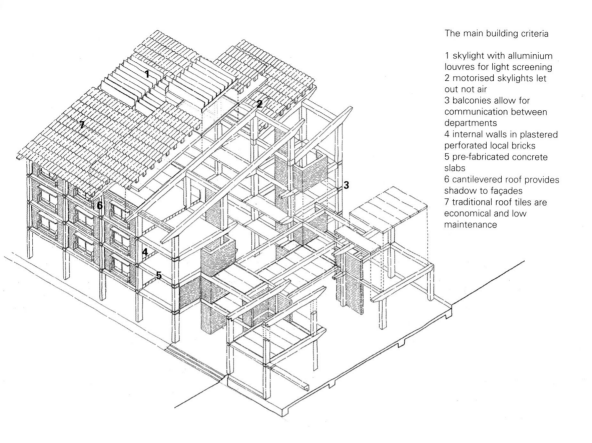

The main building criteria

1 skylight with alluminium louvres for light screening
2 motorised skylights let out not air
3 balconies allow for communication between departments
4 internal walls in plastered perforated local bricks
5 pre-fabricated concrete slabs
6 cantilevered roof provides shadow to façades
7 traditional roof tiles are economical and low maintenance

Phase 2 - The new Municipality offices

Phase 3 - The new legal offices

In conversation with Sir Michael Hopkins
Catureglio, Lucca, Italy, 2005

Did the fact that your father was a builder have any influence on your decision to study architecture? You first studied art at Bournemouth Art School and then transferred to the Architectural Association, so perhaps there was some doubt in your mind at the time. Did you want to study art at first?

Art was not in my mind at all. In fact, at Bournemouth Art School I studied architecture. I became interested in becoming an architect at school. My mother decided I was to be an architect, my brother was to be a doctor and my sister was to become an actress, and we all did! We all did exactly what we were told!

I went to boarding school in a beautiful part of England, in rural Dorset. I didn't like playing sports or working in classrooms. If you were going to be an architect you were encouraged to work in the art school, but I didn't want to do that either. I used to spend all my time on my bicycle, riding around looking at buildings in Dorset. I had a very romantic view of Dorset, through it's history and literature, which was very much tied up with the part of the countryside where my school was. That was really the beginning of my interest in architecture.

Then I went to study Architecture in the local college in Bournemouth, but I again didn't do much work because I was free, away from boarding school. Off I used to go again into the countryside. Someone, I think, called Jasper Solway used to teach history and drawing there. He was very knowledgeable about the history of Dorset and used to take us on trips. I had an old vintage 1920's car and he and I, and three or four other students, would drive off in it looking at old buildings. I might well at that point have joined the Ancient Monuments Commission. I thought that would be a really nice job to do! Old buildings were what interested me at the time.

I then worked in architectural offices in Dorset, specialising in restorations, repairing churches and schools and country houses.

Then, a proper modern architect, Frederick Gibberd, came to my hometown, Bournemouth and gave a lecture about the buildings he had designed at Harlow New Town and London Airport. And I thought this is quite different, this is really special, perhaps I should go and work in London and learn how to design buildings properly. So I went up to London and worked for him and then moved to work for Basil Spence until I was twenty-three and could get a grant independently of my parents and finally I went to study seriously at the Architectural Association and thoroughly enjoyed it.

During your years at the Architectural Association during the 1960s, you had some outstanding teachers in Peter Smithson, Cedric Price, Bob Maxwell, John Winter.

Sir Michael Hopkins

What do you remember of your education there and whose architectural thinking influenced you most then at the beginning of your career?

The Architectural Association is quite a difficult and sophisticated school to enter when you are eighteen. I was lucky that I didn't get there until I was twenty-three, so I was, personally, more confident than others straight from school. We were quite close to our teachers in age and background. I suspect Cedric Price was only a year or two older than me. At the beginning I was so enthusiastic and starved of formal education that I produced two or three schemes for every project that we were set.

We did have extraordinarily good teaching staff. At that point in time most of the tutors taught part time and worked part time as practicing architects. They were all building an interesting project, like a library or a school, or a laboratory, usually in a university town. There was not the pressure on building practice that there is now, so they could develop their own design work and teach at the same time.

Peter Smithson used to set the curriculum at the AA while I was there: he was a member of Team 10 and CIAM, so we were very influenced by the Team 10 thinking. Aldo Van Eyke, Giancarlo De Carlo were all Team 10 members. Cedric Price was very clever but not a great influence on me: he was always fun to be with.

History of architecture was extraordinarily well taught at the AA. Sir John Summerson was a lecturer. I was introduced to the Victorian Functional Tradition, a major influence on me, illustrated by the photographs of Eric De Marè. Reyner Banham taught us late nineteenth and twentieth century history, the beginning of tectonic architecture: I was very fortunate.

When we were at the AA, we weren't terribly interested in how buildings were put together or constructed, nor indeed in what they looked like. We were much more interested in how buildings came together in plan and section, and how the plan and section interpreted the social brief. Caring about the appearance of building, and how they were made, came to me through my involvement on a particular personal project.

I bought a timber frame house in Suffolk, while I was a student, for very little money and in order to repair it properly, I had to work out how it was originally put together This gave me a real insight into timber frame construction and immediately, as a flash out of the blue, I realised that there was a strong relationship between the way that buildings were put together and the way they finished up looking.

I, then, started to get interested in metal construction and began working with Norman Foster on steel frame buildings. I became very interested in the work of Charles Eames and Buckminster Fuller in America and in how they had been trying to harness various modern production techniques, as in the car component industry, and to apply those techniques to the production of buildings. This still preoccupies me.

Could you also tell us about your years with Norman Foster and your experience designing The Willis Faber and Dumas building in Ipswich?

With Norman I developed my belief in the absolute relationship between construction and built form. The Willis Faber building was a tremendous opportunity. Norman and I were only thirty-five at the time and through a process of interviews we were awarded the commission, for a very substantial building, by a very traditional old fashioned City client, who was, unusually for the time, prepared to back a modern building. And that, perhaps, is the most particular thing I remember of that period.

Buckminster Fuller once visited the house you built in Hampstead shortly after it was completed and asked the famous question "How much does it weigh?" Did you consider Buckminster Fuller a guru, as many people did, in the development of your architectural philosophy? Have you since revised your opinion of him?

Yes, Bucky visited us and yes he was a personal guru. He was an engineer who wasn't just interested in calculating things or designing bridges and viaducts. He was interested in the whole of the "built world". He was interested in taking aircraft technology and trying to convert it into industrialised housing. His mind worked very fast and it was hard to keep up with him. He was also a friend always interested in what one was doing, interested in our children and how they might develop. He described himself as a citizen of the world. He thought globally, far ahead of this time. He imagined a new world order to be based on engineering. Bucky was on the world's stage and I was very lucky to know him.

You once said, "Our architecture comes out of our engineering and our engineering comes out of our engineers". You have worked with the best engineering minds in people such as Tony Hunt, Derek Sudgen, Michael Dixon and John Thornton. What working relationship have you evolved with them over the years? How much would you say they contribute to a finished design?

Greatly. They are the first people one thinks of when one starts to build up a design team. The best ones are our philosophers. I have this recurring feeling that the best architecture grows out of the engineering, so you want the engineers in there to contribute to ideas right from the very beginning. This is not so for everybody but for me, -it is. They are also very good critics, and when you find yourself going off at a tangent and not being sufficiently rigorous; they will bring you back to the core of the matter in hand. So they do contribute enormously to our design.

A knighthood and a RIBA Gold Medal in 1994 came as the recognition of your international success. Have they in any way changed the public's perception of your work?

I don't think it "changed it", it sort of consolidated it. You become part of the architectural establishment: I am not sure this is a good thing or not!

Your architecture has often being described as quintessentially British: do you agree with this comment, and what does it actually mean for you? Is there a quintessentially British architecture at all and how would you say it transpires in your own work?

I have become increasingly interested in the idea of a building growing out of it's physical context, whatever the sort of building. It may not be an obvious context and the end result might look extremely unusual, as our Schulmberger Cambridge Research Centre. Here the programme demanded a large shed, housing oil-drilling equipment. How does one handle that on the site, a flat plain outside Cambridge? There were only two other buildings on the skyline, Kings College Chapel and the University Library. So we gave it a form that responded to it's function, but we made the form out of a white membrane, so that it undulates like white clouds in the sky. It is still very successful.

I didn't travel abroad very much when I was younger but spent a lot of time in the English countryside and in English towns, so I have a strong feeling for those. When you find yourself working in Italy, you look at Italian landscape and Italian towns: you adjust. Apart from our villa here at Catureglio, we have not actually built anything in Italy, although we have produced a lot of schemes. Here at Catureglio I have approached the restoration in the same way I would have approached it in Britain: to repair and slightly extend these buildings, so they became seamless part of this landscape: it is a way of putting things back together and thinking about things…

So, in a way, contextual thinking is a mark of "Britishness" that, for me, goes back to my education in the Dorset countryside. But, it is also a mark of good architecture, not just British.

You have worked for very prestigious clients (such as the Crown, Parliament, the University of Cambridge, Yale, Princeton), what was it they were attracted to in your firm – or perhaps in your architecture?

I think it is an ability to find the particular Zeitgeist of the place where you are working and then reinterpret it freshly for the particular problem on hand.

You own a beautiful villa near Lucca and are also working on various projects in Italy. You have also worked in Athens. How would you compare the state of architectural design in England and the Continent?

I am not sure about the Continent as a whole. In England we are educated to expect to design new buildings. While I get the feeling in Italy, apart from a small number of exceptions, that you train a huge number of architects, that is a very enjoyable training to do, but that they don't necessarily have the expectation of going on to design new buildings. There is so much old fabric in Italy to care for. The sad thing is that, even when there is a new building to design, an Italian architect is not automatically employed to do it! I find Italian building confusing at the moment: there is such an innate feeling for design and engineering, but it doesn't always manifest itself in new architecture: strange.

Some years ago, while designing the Inland Revenue Centre in Nottingham, you told me that sustainable architecture was still in its infancy. How much has it progressed since then and how much influence will it have in your future designs?

Its influence is increasing all the time. In the same way that the expression of the structure of our buildings always played an important part in their design in the past, now how our buildings appear, how they are perceived, what they look like, what they are made out of, is increasingly going to depend on their environmental engineering, which is the basis of sustainable architecture.

You have been described as both a "problem solver" and an innovator. You have updated the language of traditional materials with innovative results (the use of the brick/stone pier is a prime example). Where will your architecture go from here?

We are beginning to develop a new language out of our environmental strategies. I'm certain that ongoing investigations into the possibilities of sustainable systems will increasingly influence our architecture. In our office the younger generation are leading on environmental design, they are the ones that got me interested in it's potential. And I am now starting to think of ways to develop and incorporate it, not just to achieve buildings with very high-energy ratings, but also to use it in ways that it actually changes our architecture. We are beginning to develop a new architectural language out of our environmental strategies.

Selected Bibliography

General publications

Colin Davis, *Hopkins: The Work of Michael Hopkins and Partners,* Phaidon Press, London 1993
Colin Davis, *Hopkins 2: The work of Michael Hopkins and Partners,* Phaidon Press, London 2001
Todd Willmert, "The Return of Natural Ventilation", *Architectural Record,* July 2001

Projects

Hopkins' House, London, 1975–76
John Winter, *House in Hampstead,* "Architectural Review", December 1977

Schlumberger Cambridge Research Centre, 1990–92
Henry Herzberg, "High Flyer", *Architects' Journal,* 24 October 1984
Patrick Hannay, "A Glimpse of Tomorrow", *Architects' Journal,* 15 May 1985
Stephen Groak, "A Cambridge Test: Hopkins for Schlumberger", *Architects' Journal,* 18 September 1985
John Winter and Sarah Jackson, "Technology Stretching High-Tech", *Architects' Journal,* 18 October 1992

Mound Stand, Lord's Cricket Ground, London, 1984–87
Scoring High Hopkins at Lord's', "Architects' Journal", 2 September 1987
David Jenkins, *The Mound Stand: Lord's Cricket Ground,* Phaidon Press, London 1991

Bracken House, London 1987–92
Colin Avery, *Bracken House,* Wordsearch Publishing, 1992
Patrick Hodgkinson, "Classic Support?", Gothic Phoenix, *Architectural Review,* May 1992

David Mellor Cutlery Factory, Hathersage, 1988–89
Kenneth Murta, "Design at the Cutting Edge", *RIBA Journal,* October 1998

David Mellor Offices and Showroom, London, 1988–91
Frances Anderton, "Architecture for All Senses", *Architectural Review,* October 1991

Glyndebourne Opera House, Sussex, 1989–94
Marcus Binney and Rosy Runciman, *Glyndebourne - Building a Vision,* Thames and Hudson, London 1994
Mark Swenarton, "Arcadian Overtures", *Architecture Today,* May 1994
Colin Davies, "Glyndebourne", *Architectural Review,* June 1994

Portcullis House, New Parliamentary Building, London, 1989–2000
"Mother Nature", *ECO,* June 1997
Mark Swenerton, "Heart of Oak: Timber Engineering at Portcullis House", *Architecture Today,* June 1999
Katherine Bateson, "Happy Campus", *Building Design,* 9 June 2000
Hugh Pearman, "The House next Door", *The Sunday Times,* 6 August 2000

John Thornton, "The New Parliamentary Building: Portcullis House", *The Structural Engineer,* 19 September 2000
Peter Davey, "Common Sense", *Architectural Review,* February 2001

Dynamic Earth, Edinburgh, 1990–99
Brian Edwards, "Michael Hopkins' Dynamic Earth heads the regeneration of Edinburgh's east end", *Architecture Today,* February 2000

Westminster Underground Station, London, 1990–99
Martin Pawley, "Going Underground", *Architects' Journal,* 3 February 2000
Penny McGuire, "Underneath the Politics", *Architectural Review,* June 2000
Kenneth Powell, "The Jubilee Line Extension", *Westminster Underground Station,* October 2000

Inland Revenue Centre, Nottingham, 1992–95
Peter Davey, "Raising the Revenue", *Architectural Review,* May 1995

Queen's Building, Emmanuel College, Cambridge, 1993–95
Colin Davies, "Cambridge Credo", *Architectural Review,* February 1996

Buckingham Palace Ticket Office, London, 1994–95
Deborah Singmaster, "Summer themes welcomes visitors to the Palace", *Architects' Journal,* 8 September 1994

Manchester Art Gallery, 1994–2002
Raymund Ryan, "Discreet Charm", *RIBA Journal,* June 2002

The Forum, Norwich, 1994–2002
Jay Merrick, "Norwich's Glass Act", *The Independant,* 8 November 2001
Nick Jones, *New Learning Hub, ABC&D,* November 2001

Norwich Cathedral Refectory, 1995–2004
Marcus Binney, *The Times,* June 2004
Jay Merrick, *The Independent,* June 2004
Eleanor Young, "Keep The Faith", *RIBA Journal,* June 2004

Jubilee Campus, University of Nottingham, 1996–99
Campus Arcadia, *Architectural Review,* February 2000
"Green Agenda: Hopkins and Partners at Nottingham", *Architecture Today EcoTech Supplement,* March 2000
Martin Pearce, *University Builders,* Wiley-Academy, 2001

Haberdashers' Hall, London, 1996–2002
Peter Fawcett, "City and Guild", *Architects' Journal,* July 2002

Goodwood Racecourse, Sussex, 1997–2001
Peter Davey, "Glorious Goodwood", *Architectural Review,* February 2002

Inn the Park, St. James' Park, London, 1998–2004

Exhibitions

Amanda Bailieu, "Hidden Treasure", *RIBA Journal,* June 2004

The Wellcome Trust Gibbs Building, London, 1999–2004
Hugh Pearman, "His light materials", *The Sunday Times,* January 2005
Kenneth Powell, "Wellcome Home", *Architectural Review,* February 2005
Elaine Knutt, *FX Magazine,* March 2005
"Structural Steel Design Awards Winner", *New Steel Construction,* July/August 2005

Evelina Children's Hospital, London, 1999–2005
Peter Scher, "South Bank Show", *Hospital Development,* March 2005
Paul Finch, "Light Touch", *Architectural Review,* May 2005
Martin Spring, "Open Air Surgery", *Building magazine,* 10 June 2005
"Children Help Create Hospital", *New Steel Construction,* 1st November 2005
Stephen Kennett, "A Breath of Fresh Air", *Building Services Journal,* 1st November 2005
Hugh Pearman, "Just What the Doctor Ordered", *The Sunday Times,* 20 November 2005
Luca Maria Francesco Fabris, "Colori Salutari", *Costruire,* November 2005
Louis Jebb, "This Won't Hurt a Bit", *The Independent,* 1st November 2005
Eleanor Young, "Just what the doctor ordered", *RIBA Journal,* December 2005

1985
Exhibition on Industrial Architecture, University of Stuttgart

1987
Royal Academy Exhibition, London

1990
UIA Congress Exhibition

1991
Royal Fine Art Commission, retrospective exhibition

1992
Westminster Underground Jubilee Line Exhibition (co-ordinated by the Architecture Foundation)
Prince Philip Prize for Designer of the Year Exhibition

1994
RIBA Competitions 1984-1994
RIBA Royal Gold Medal Exhibition, The work of Michael Hopkins and Partners
Exhibitions in The Herron Gallery, School of Architecture, University of East London

1995
Steel Houses, RIBA Heinz Gallery
The Buckminster Fuller Centennial Exhibition - Contemporary Developments in Design Science, New York
Tate Gallery for Modern Art: Selecting an Architect
'Making Space for Theatre' British Theatre Architecture Exhibition (co-ordinated by the British Council)
Saudi Arabia and Britain – Partners in Progress

(organised by the Design Museum on behalf of the DTI)
Architects' Journal Centenary Exhibition
Best of British Design (Design Museum Exhibition in Johannesburg)

1996
Contemporary British Architects, National Academy of Design, New York
Wood in Contemporary Architecture Exhibition, France
Design Futures: New British Design and Architecture, Prague
RIBA Awards for Architecture 1996

1997
Picking Winners – RIBA Exhibition
Drawing on Diversity: women, architecture and practice (RIBA)

1998
New Urban Environments - British Architecture in a European Context, Tokyo
12 for 2000 – Building for the Millennium (exhibition of the British Council)

1999
Quay Designs, Arnolfini Gallery, Bristol
Architecture of Democracy 1999–2000, Glasgow, Manchester, Dublin
Theatre Architecture, Prague Quadrienalle

2000
Ten Shades of Green, USA tour
Westminster 2000 - Fair in the Square, London
SAIE 2000, Bologna, Italy
Royal Institute of British

Architects Transport by Design Exhibition

2001
Architetture a Confronto, Mantova, Italy
Royal Academy Summer Exhibition, London
Royal Academy New Connections Exhibition, New York
Component Design, Building Centre, London

2002
Royal Academy Summer Exhibition, London

2002–2003
Green Giants Exhibition, Washington, USA
Royal Academy Summer Exhibition, London

2004
Venice Biennale, Italy
SAIE, Bologna, Italy
Royal Academy Summer Exhibition, London

2005
Royal Academy Summer Exhibition, London
Evelina Children's Hospital Exhibition, Royal Institute of British Architects, London
Capital Health, New London Architecture Gallery, London
London Lights, New London Architecture Gallery, London

2006
Royal Academy Summer Exhibition, London

Awards

Bracken House, London
1992
RIBA Award
City Heritage Award
British Construction Industry
Award
1993
Financial Times Architecture
Award
1994
Civic Trust Award

**David Mellor Cutlery
Factory, Hathersage,
Sheffield**
1989
RIBA Award
Financial Times Architecture
Award
1990
Civic Trust Award
BBC Design Award

**David Mellor Offices
and Showroom, London,**
1993
RIBA Award

Dubai Marina Towers
2004
Cityscape Architectural
Review Future Projects
Award, Dubai

**Evelina Children's
Hospital, London**
2005
Built in Quality Award
2006
Civic Trust Award
RIBA Award

**GEK-Terna Headquarters,
Athens**
2004
RIBA Award

**Glyndebourne Opera
House, Sussex**
1994
RIBA Award
Supreme Brick Award
Royal Fine Art Commission
Trust Millennium Building

of the Year Award
British Construction Industry
Award
1995
Civic Trust Award
Financial Times Building
of the Year Award
1996
USITT Architecture Award
Honour Award

**Goodwood Racecourse,
Sussex**
2001
Industrial Fabrics
Association International
Outstanding Achievement
for Air & Tension Structures
2003
Civic Trust Award
2005
IAKS Award

**Haberdashers' Hall,
London**
2002
The Company of Chartered
Architects con City Heritage
Society New Building Award
2003
Wood Award
2005
The Worshipful Company
of Tylers and Bricklayers'
Triennal Award

Hopkins House, London
1977
RIBA Award
1979
Civic Trust Award

**Inland Revenue Centre,
Nottingham**
1995
Brick Award for the Best
Commercial and Industrial
Building
International Prize for Textile
Architecture
1996
Concrete Society Award
Highly Commended Green
Building of Year Award

1997
Civic Trust Energy Award
Conservation Award
1999
IOC/IAKS Award for
Exemplary Sports and
Leisure Facilities

**Inn the Park, St. James'
Park, London**
2004
Wood Award
BD Architect of the
Year Award (Leisure
category)
2005
Time Out, London Eating
& Drinking Awards category
Westminster Society
Award
2006
Civic Trust Award

**Jubilee Campus,
University of Nottingham**
2000
British Construction Industry
Award
Nottingham Lord Mayor's
Award
2001
RIBA Award
RIBA Journal Sustainability
Award
2001
UK Solar Award
2002
Energy Globe Award
Civic Trust Award for
Sustainability
2005
RICS Award, Sustainability

**Jubilee Line extension,
London**
2000
Civic Trust Award
British Construction
Industry Award

Manchester Art Gallery
2002
Civic Society of Manchester
Phoenix Award

2003
Royal Fine Art Commission
Trust Award
RIBA Award
Concrete Society Award
2004
Civic Trust Award

**Mound Stand, Lord's
Cricket Ground, London,**
1988
RIBA Award
Civic Trust Award
1991
IOC/IAKS Award

**National College School
Leadership**
2003
RIBA East Midlands Award

**New Square, Bedfont
Lakes, London**
1993
Financial Times Architecture
Award
Structural Steel Award

**Northern Arizona
University Advance
Research and
Development Facility,
Flagstaff, USA**
2005
Holcim Awards
Acknowledgement 2005

**Norwich Cathedral
Refectory**
2004
Wood Award, Gold Award
Architect of the Year Award
2005
Royal Fine Art Commission
Trust, Building of the Year
RIBA Award
Civic Trust Award

**Portcullis House, New
Parliamentary Building,
London**
2001
Institute of Structural
Engineers David

Credits

Alsop Award
RIBA Award
The Copper in Architecture
Awards 9 – Architectural
Design Innovation Award
Timber Industry Award
Concrete Society Award
2002
European Concrete
Society Network Building
Prize
Civic Trust Award
Natural Stone Award
2003
Westminster Society Award

Queen's Building, Emmanuel College, Cambridge
1996
RIBA Award
1996
RIBA Architecture in
Education Award
Royal Fine Art Commission
Trust Building of the Year
1997
Natural Stone Award - New
Build Category Award
Carpenters Award 1997

Schlumberger Cambridge Research Centre (phase 1)
1988
RIBA Award
Civic Trust Award
1985
Financial Times Architecture
Award
Structural Steel Award

Schlumberger Cambridge Research Centre (phase 2)
1993
RIBA Award
Financial Times Architecture
Award

The Forum, Norwich
2003
Civic Trust Award
2004
RIBA Award
Brick Award

The Wellcome Trust Gibbs Building, London
2005
RIBA Award
Structural Steel Awards
2006
Art and Work Awards,
Outstanding Contribution
to Art in the Working
Environment

"Utopia" Broughton Hall, Yorkshire
2006
RIBA Award

Westminster Underground Station, London
2000
Royal Fine Art Commission
Trust Millennium Building
of the Year Award
2001
RIBA Award
Concrete Society Award
2002
European Concrete Society
Network Building Prize
Civic Trust Award
2003
Westminster Society Award

Hopkins House, London
1975–76

Architect
Hopkins Architects

Hopkins Design Team
Sir Michael Hopkins, Lady
Patricia Hopkins

Structural Engineer
Anthony Hunt Associates

Greene King Brewery Draught Beer Cellars, Bury St Edmunds, Suffolk
1977–80

Client
Greene King plc

Architect
Hopkins Architects

Hopkins Design Team
Sir Michael Hopkins, John
Pringle, Ian Sharratt, David
Harris, Mark Sutcliffe, Chris
Wilkinson

Structural Engineer
Anthony Hunt Associates

Services Engineer
R.W. Gregory & Partners

Main Contractor
Bovis Construction Ltd

Quantity Surveyor
Davis Belfield & Everest

Patera Building System and Hopkins Studio, London
1980–82

Client
Patera Productions Ltd

Architect
Hopkins Architects

Hopkins Design Team
Sir Michael Hopkins, John
Pringle, Peter Romaniuk,
David Allsop, Chris
Williamson

Structural Engineer
Anthony Hunt Associates

Services Engineer
Dale & Goldfinger

*Fire and Engineer
Consultant*
Ove Arup & Partners

Schlumberger Cambridge Research Centre (phase 1)
1982–85

Client
Schlumberger Cambridge
Research Ltd

Architect
Hopkins Architects

Hopkins Design Team
Sir Michael Hopkins, John
Pringle, Chris Williamson,
Nic Bewick, Robin Snell,
John Eger

Structural Engineer
Anthony Hunt Associates
Ove Arup & Partners

Services Engineer
YRM Engineers

Quantity Surveyor
Davis Belfield & Everest

Acoustic consultant
Tim Smith Acoustics

Fire consultant
Ove Arup & Partners

Main Contractor
Bovis Construction Ltd

Quantity Surveyor
White & Turner

Schlumberger Cambridge Research Centre (phase 2)
1990–92

Client
Schlumberger Cambridge
Research Ltd

Architect
Hopkins Architects

Hopkins Design Team
Sir Michael Hopkins, John
Pringle, James Greaves,
Alan Jones, Annabel Hollick,
Tom Emerson

Structural Engineer
Buro Happold

Services Engineer
Buro Happold

Quantity Surveyors
Davis Langdon & Everest

Main Contractor
Team Management
(Southern) Ltd

PVC Canopy design
Buro Happold

**Fleet Velmead Infants
School, Hampshire**
1984–86

Client
Hampshire County Council

Architect
Hopkins Architects

Hopkins Design Team
Sir Michael Hopkins, Lady
Patricia Hopkins, Sheila
Thompson, Bill Dunster

*Structural and Services
Engineer*
Buro Happold

Main Contractor
Wates Construction
(Southern)

Quantity Surveyor
Davis Belfield & Everest

**Mound Stand, Lord's
Cricket Ground, London**
1984–87

Client
Marylebone Cricket Club

Architect
Hopkins Architects

Hopkins Design Team
Sir Michael Hopkins, John
Pringle, William Taylor,
Ernest Fasanya, Andrew
Barnett, David Selby, David
Sparrow, Chris Thurlbourne,
Simon Herron

*Structural and Services
Engineer*
Ove Arup & Partners

Quantity Surveyor
David Langdon & Everest

Fire Consultant
Ove Arup & Partners

Main Contractor
John Lelliott Ltd

**Solid State Logic,
Begbroke, Oxon**
1986–88

Client
Solid State Logic

Architect
Hopkins Architects

Hopkins Design Team
Sir Michael Hopkins, Ian
Sharratt, Peter Romaniuk,
Peter Cartwright, Bill
Dunster, Graham Saunders

*Structural and Services
Engineer*
Buro Happold

Quantity Surveyor
Davis Langdon & Everest

Main Contractor
Walter Lawrence Project
Management

Bracken House, London
1987–92

Client
Obayashi Corporation
Europe BV

Architect
Hopkins Architects

Hopkins Design Team
Sir Michael Hopkins, John
Pringle, David Selby, Robin
Snell, Bill Dunster, Patrick
Nee, Andrew Barnett, Arif
Mehmood, Helena Webster,
Emma Nsugbe, Allessando
Calafati, Ernest Fasanya,
Emma Adams, Loretta
Gentilini, Marki Kuwayama,
Mike Eleftheriades, Colin
Muir, Neno Kezic, Tommaso
del Buono, Nicholas
Boyarsky, Gail Halvorsen,
Amir Sanei, Robert Bishop,
Margaret Leong, Nick
Malby, Pippa Nissen, Joao
Passanha, Oriel Prizeman,
Sundeep Singh Bhamra,
Ameer Bin Tahir, Chris
Thurlbourne, Jim Dunster,
Boon Yang Sim, Charles
Webster, Sanya Polescuk,
Gina Raimi

*Structural and Services
Engineer*
Ove Arup & Partners

Quantity Surveyor
Northcroft Neighbour
& Nicholson

Construction Consultant
Schal International Ltd

Fire consultant
Arup Research
& Development

Acoustic Consultant
Arup Acoustics

Main Contractor
Trollope & Colls
Construction Ltd

**David Mellor Cutlery
Factory, Hathersage,
Sheffield**
1988–89

Client
David Mellor Design Ltd

Architect
Hopkins Architects

Hopkins Design Team
Sir Michael Hopkins, John
Pringle, Bill Dunster, Neno
Kezic

Structural Engineer
Whitby Bird

Main Contractor
David Mellor Design Ltd

**David Mellor Offices and
Showroom, London**
1988–91

Client
David Mellor Design Limited

Architect
Hopkins Architects

Hopkins Team
Sir Michael Hopkins, John
Pringle, Bill Dunster, Ernest
Fasanya, Lucy Lavers, Neno
Kezic

*Structural and Services
Engineer*
Buro Happold

Contractor
Sir Robert McAlpine
Management Contracting
Limited
David Mellor Design Ltd

**New Square, Bedfont
Lakes, London**
1989–92

Client
MEPC/IBM Joint Venture

Architect
Hopkins Architects

Hopkins Design Team
Sir Michael Hopkins, Ian
Sharratt, Peter Romaniuk,
Pamela Bate, Peter
Cartwright, Brendan Phelan,
Jane Willoughby, Stephen
Macbean, Gerhard Landau,
Dominique Gagnon, Susan
Hillberg, Marybeth
McTeague, Andy Young,
Chin Lai, Tommaso del

Buono, John Hoepfner,
Michael Wentworth,
Danielle Mantelin, Clare
Endicott

Structural & Fire Engineers
Buro Happold

Services Engineer
FHP Partnership

Quantity Surveyors
Bucknall Austin

Main Contractor
Costain Construction Ltd

Acoustic Consultant
Moir Hands & Associates

Landscape Consultant
Land Use Consultants

**Glyndebourne Opera
House, Sussex**
1989–94

Client
Glyndebourne Productions
Ltd

Architect
Hopkins Architects

Hopkins Directors
Sir Michael Hopkins, Lady
Patricia Hopkins

Hopkins Associates
Andrew Barnett, Pamela
Bate, Robin Snell

Hopkins Design Team
Justin Bere, Tommasomo
del Buono, Peter Cartwright,
Nigel Curry, Jim Dunster,
Alison Fisher, Loretta
Gentilini, Julie Hamilton,
Lucy Lavers, Anif
Mehmood, Margaret
Mitchell, Emma Nsugbe,
Kevin O'Sullivan, Martin
Pease, Claire Tarbard, Mark
Turkel, Andrew Wells,
Edward Williams

Quantity Surveyors
Gardiner & Theobold

Engineers
Ove Arup & Partners

Acoustic Consultant
Arup Acoustics

Construction Manager
Bovis Construction

Theatre Consultants
Theatre Project Consultants

**Portcullis House, New
Parliamentary Building
and Westminster
Underground Station,
London**

1989–2000

Client
House of Commons, Accommodation & Works Committee

Architect
Hopkins Architects

Hopkins Directors
Sir Michael Hopkins, Lady Patricia Hopkins, Pamela Bate, John Pringle, Peter Romaniuk, David Selby

Hopkins Associates
Bill Dunster, Steven MacBean, Patrick Nee, Brendan Phelan, Robin Snell

Hopkins Design Team
Emma Adams, Suzanne Bach, Chris Bannister, Toby Birtwistle, Robert Bishop, Rebecca Chipchase, Gary Collins, Martyn Corner, Paul Cutler, Cormac Deavy, Neil Eaton, Alison Fisher, Simon Fraser, Julian Gitsham, Mark Greene, Gail Halvorsen, Steve Harris, Buddy Haward, Margaret Leong, Phillipp Metternich-Sandor, Vanitie Mossman, Anna Radcliffe, Amaani Raimi, Mark Robinson, Amir Sanei, Alex Small, Jenny Stevens, Tom Stevens, Alex Sykes, Michael Taylor, Taro Tsuruta, Peter Unga, Angus Waddington, Tony White, Hannah Wooller, Andy Young

Structural Engineer
Arup: John Thornton, Dervilla Mitchell

Building Services Engineer
Arup & Partners: John Berry

Façade Engineering
Arup & Partners: Neil Noble, Andrew Hall

Quantity Surveyors
Gardiner & Theobald: Roger Fidgen, Stewart Whittle

Project Management
Schal International Management Ltd: Roy Davis, David Verity

Construction Management
Laing Management Ltd: Andy Lowther, Simon Harding

Tottenham Court Road Station, London
1990–

Client
London Regional Transport

Architect
Hopkins Architects

Hopkins Design Team
Sir Michael Hopkins, William Taylor, James Greaves, Patrick Nee, Ben Fereday, Simon Fraser, Lydia Haack, Georgina Hall, Julie Hamilton

Structural and Services Engineer
Ove Arup & Partners

Quantity Surveyor
Franklin Andrews

Dynamic Earth, Edinburgh
1990–99

Client
Lothian & Edinburgh Enterprise Ltd (LEEL)

Architect
Hopkins Architects

Hopkins Directors
Sir Michael Hopkins, Lady Patricia Hopkins, James Greaves, Ian Sharratt

Hopkins Project Director
Annabel Hollick

Hopkins Design Team
Meriel Blackburn, Martyn Corner, Ben Cousins, Alison Fisher, Daniel Fugenschuh, Andrew Morrison, Gerard Page, Andrew Stanway, Sarah Thomson, Jane Willoughby, Andrew Young

Quantity Surveyor
Gardiner & Theobold

Project Management
Kier Project Management (ex-TEAM)

Main Contractor
Laing Management (Scotland) Ltd

Engineers
Ove Arup and Partners

Leisure Consultant
Grant Leisure Group

Acoustic Consultant
Robin Mackenzie Partnership

Inland Revenue Centre, Nottingham
1992–95

Client
Inland Revenue

Architect
Hopkins Architects

Hopkins Directors
Sir Michael Hopkins, Ian Sharratt, William Taylor

Hopkins Associates
Pamela Bate, Peter Romaniuk, Brendan Phelan, Bill Dunster, Stephen Macbean

Hopkins Design Team
Nathan Barr, Russell Baylis, Peter Cartwright, Max Connop, Jason Cooper, Paul Cutler, Ernest Fasanya, Alison Fisher, Simon Fraser, Lydia Haack, Alan Jones, Jonathan Knight, Amanda Lanchbery, Catherine Martin, Carol Painter, Brian Reynolds, Guni Suri, Claire Tarbard, Charles Walker

Engineers
Ove Arup & Partners

Client Project Manager
Turner & Townsend Project Management

Quantity Surveyors
Turner & Townsend

Main Contractor
Laing Management Ltd

Acoustic Consultants
Arup Acoustics

Queen's Building, Emmanuel College, Cambridge
1993–95

Client
Emmanuel College

Architect
Hopkins Architects

Hopkins Directors
Sir Michael Hopkins, Lady Patricia Hopkins

Hopkins Senior Associate
James Greaves

Hopkins Design Team
Alison Fisher, Buddy Haward, Alex Mowat, Michael Taylor, Mark Turkel

Structural and Services Engineer
Buro Happold

Main Contractor
Sir Robert McAlpine

Quantity Surveyor
Davis Langdon & Everest

Lady Sarah Cohen House, London
1993–96

Client
Community Trading Ltd

Architect
Hopkins Architects

Hopkins Directors
Sir Michael Hopkins, Lady Patricia Hopkins

Hopkins Associates
Andrew Barnett, Pamela Bate

Hopkins Design Team
Jim Dunster, Alison Fisher, Steve Harris, Ken Hood, Abigail Hopkins, Lucy Lavers, Arif Mehmood, Yale Melameade, Ian Milne, Andy Wells, Edward Williams, Jane Willoughby

Structural Engineer
Jampel Davison & Bell

Main Contractor
Try Build Ltd

Quantity Surveyor
Basil Cohen

Buckingham Palace Ticket Office, London
1994–95

Client
Royal Collection Enterprises Limited

Architect
Hopkins Architect

Hopkins Directors
Sir Michael Hopkins, William Taylor

Hopkins Project Director
Jonathan Knight

Hopkins Design Team
Susan Cox, Alison Fisher, Andrew Jordan, Annabel Judd, Jenny Stevens

Consultant Structural Engineer
Ove Arup & Partners

Construction Manager
Laing Management Limited

Main Contractor
Holloway White Allom Limited

Roofing Consultant
Landrell

Joinery Consultant
Cheeseman Interiors

Sheltered Housing, Charterhouse, London
1994–2000

Client
The Governors of Suttons Hospital in Charterhouse

Architect
Hopkins Architects

Hopkins Directors
Sir Michael Hopkins, Lady Patricia Hopkins, James Greaves

Hopkins Associates
Brendan Phelan, Arif Mehmood

Hopkins Design Team
Martyn Corner, Alison Fisher, Simon French, Chris Gray, Buddy Haward, Sarah Thomson, Sophy Twohig

Structural and Services Engineer
Buro Happold

Main Contractor
Eve Construction

Quantity Surveyor
Davis Langdon & Everest

Hampshire County Cricket Club, Southampton
1994–2001

Client
Hampshire County Cricket Club

Architect
Hopkins Architects

Hopkins Directors
Sir Michael Hopkins, William Taylor, Peter Romaniuk, Pamela Bate

Hopkins Project Director
Ernest Fasanya, Tim Sloan

Hopkins Design Team
Stefanie Arnold, Kate Ashurst, Stuart Blower, Susan Cox, Alison Fisher, Stephen Fletcher, David Fox, Spencer Guy, Matthew Hoad, Andrew Jordan, Tobias Lossing, Stephen Macbean, Jan Mackie, Kristi Roger, Arifa Salim, Rud Sawers, Jenny Stevens, Paul Vick

Engineers
Buro Happold

Main Contractor
P Trant Ltd

Quantity Surveyor
Denley King & Partners

Manchester Art Gallery
1994–2002

Client
Manchester City Council

Architect
Hopkins Architects

Hopkins Directors
Sir Michael Hopkins, Lady Patricia Hopkins, William Taylor, David Selby

Hopkins Project Director
Jonathan Knight, Arif Mehmood

Hopkins Design Team
Kate Ashurst, Shahid Chaudry, Martyn Corner, Alison Fisher, Alex Franz, Robert Gregory, Spencer Guy, Caroline Hislop, Lydia Kan, Stephen Luxford, David Merllie, Gina Raimi, Paul Segers, Gabby Shawcross, Tim Sloan, Alexandra Small, Jenny Stevens, Sonja Stoffels, Sophie Ungerer, Andrew Wood

Structural and Services Engineer
Ove Arup & Partners

Main Contractor
Bovis Construction Ltd

Quantity Surveyor
Gardiner & Theobald

The Pilkington Laboratories, Sherborne School, Dorset
1995–2000

Client
Sherborne School

Architect
Hopkins Architects

Hopkins Directors
Sir Michael Hopkins, Lady Patricia Hopkins, James Greaves

Hopkins Design Team
Alison Fisher, Jane Greaves, Andrew Morrison, Andrew Stanway, Sarah Thomson, Therese Wendland

Structural and Services Engineer
Anthony Ward Partnership

Main Contractor
Woodpecker Properties Ltd

Quantity Surveyor
Davis Langdon & Everest

Wildscreen@Bristol
1995–2000

Client
@t Bristol Ltd

Architect
Hopkins Architects

Hopkins Directors
Sir Michael Hopkins, Lady Patricia Hopkins, Andrew Barnett, James Greaves

Hopkins Project Director
Edward Williams

Hopkins Design Team
Gary Clark, Martyn Corner, Natasha Cox, Julie Gaulter, Tom Holdom, Alison Fisher, Claire Fleetwood, Caroline Hislop, Martin Knight, Henry Kong, Aikiri Paing, Jenny Stevens, Tim Whiteley

Structural and Services Engineer
Buro Happold

Services Engineer
Buro Happold

Main Contractor
Bovis Construction Ltd

Quantity Surveyor
Davis Langdon & Everest

Norwich Cathedral Refectory, Norwich (Phase 1)
1995–2004

Client
The Dean and Chapter of Norwich Cathedral

Architect
Hopkins Architects

Hopkins Directors
Sir Michael Hopkins, Andrew Barnett, Michael Taylor

Hopkins Project Director
Ken Hood

Hopkins Design Team
Gary Collins, Martyn Corner, Bruce Fisher, Emma Frater, Stephen Jones, Henry Kong, Amy Napier, Aikari Paing, Sophy Twohig, Tim Whiteley

Project Manager
Gardiner Theobald Management Services

Structural Engineer
Buro Happold

Services Engineer
Buro Happold

Main Contractor
RG Carter, Norwich

Quantity Surveyor
Davis Langdon and Everest

Saga Group Headquarters, Folkestone
1996–98

Client
Saga Group Ltd

Architect
Hopkins Architects

Hopkins Directors
Sir Michael Hopkins, Ian Sharratt, William Taylor,

Hopkins Senior Associates
Pamela Bate, Brendan Phelan

Hopkins Project Director
Michael Taylor, Arif Mehmood

Hopkins Design Team
Jonh Buck, Paul Cutler, Martyn Corner, Matthew Driscoll, Alison Fisher, Simon French, Chris Gray, Lydia Haack, Buddy Haward, Abigail Hopkins, Alan Jones, Stephen Jones, Andrew Jordan, Annabel Judd, Amanda Lanchberry, Taro Tsuruta, Sophy Twohig

Engineers
Ove Arup & Partners

Construction Manager
Schal

Project Manager
Davis Langdon Management

Quantity Surveyor
Davis Langdon & Everest

Jubilee Campus, University of Nottingham, Jubilee Campus (Phase 1)
1996–99

Client
University of Nottingham

Architect
Hopkins Architects

Hopkins Directors
Sir Michael Hopkins, William Taylor, Pamela Bate, Simon Fraser

Hopkins Project Directors
Bill Dunster, Jan Mackie

Hopkins Design Team
Martyn Corner, Alison Fisher, Steve Harris, Matthew Hoad, Toki

Hoshino, Steve Mason, Uli Moeller, Gina Raimi, Rachel Sayers, Jenny Stevens, Eric Svenkerund, Alex Sykes

Structural and Services Engineer
Ove Arup & Partners

Main Contractor
Bovis Construction Ltd

Quantity Surveyor
Gardiner & Theobald

National College for School Leadership, Nottingham (Phase 2)
2000–02

Client
University of Nottingham

Architect
Hopkins Architects

Hopkins Directors
Sir Michael Hopkins, William Taylor, Simon Fraser

Hopkins Project Director
Jan Mackie

Hopkins Design Team
Andrew Ardill, Martyn Corner, Matthew Hoad, Sophie Histon, Stephen Luxford, Steve Mason, Arifa Salim, Pascale Schulte

Structural and Services Engineer
Ove Arup & Partners

Main Contractor
Laing Management Ltd

Quantity Surveyor
Gardiner & Theobald

The Forum, Norwich, Norfolk
1996–2001

Client
Norfolk and Norwich Millennium Co Ltd

Architect
Hopkins Architects

Hopkins Directors
Sir Michael Hopkins, William Taylor, David Selby

Hopkins Project Directors
Michael Taylor, Jonathan Knight

Hopkins Design Team
Stuart Blower, Barbara Campbell-Lange, Laura Carrara-Cagni, Gary Clark, Martyn Corner, Dan Dorell, Bruce Fisher, Alison Fisher, Claire Fleetwood, Chris

Gray, Spencer Guy, Abigail Hopkins, Will Kavanagh, Mark Hatter, Martin Kaefer, Martin Knight, Ken McAndrew, Arifa Salim, Jenny Stevens, Sophy Twohig, John Vine

Project Management
Davis Langdon & Everest

Quantity Surveyor
Turner & Townsend

Structural Engineer
Whitby Bird & Partners

Services Engineer
Oscar Faber Group Ltd

Main Contractor
R G Carter Ltd

Lighting Consultant
Eric Maddock

Fire Consultant
Jeremy Gardner Associates

Acoustics
Adrian James Associates

Theatre Consultants
Event Communications

Haberdashers' Hall, London
1996–2002

Client
The Haberdashers' Company

Architect
Hopkins Architects

Hopkins Directors
Sir Michael Hopkins, Lady Patricia Hopkins, James Greaves

Hopkins Design Team
Meriel Blackburn, Chris Gray, Jack Hosea, Andrew Morrison, Amir Sanei, Andrew Stanway, Sarah Thomson, Therese Wendland, Tony White

Structural and Services Engineer
Ove Arup & Partners

Main Contractor
Holloway White Allom

Quantity Surveyor
Robinson Low Francis

Goodwood Racecourse, Sussex
1997–2001

Client
Goodwood Racecourse Ltd

Architect
Hopkins Architects

Hopkins Directors
Sir Michael Hopkins, James Greaves, Edward Williams

Hopkins Design Team
Ashu Chathley, Martyn Corner, Carsten Czaja, Chris Gray, Caroline Hislop, James Reader, John Ridgett, Andrew Stanway, Therese Wendland

Structural and Services Engineer
Ove Arup & Partners

Project Manager
Gardiner and Theobald Management Services

Quantity Surveyor
Gardiner and Theobald Management Services

Main Contractor
John Mowlem and Company plc

Mechanical and Electrical Services
Semple Cochrane plc

Inn the Park, St. James' Park, London
1998–2004

Client
The Royal Parks Agency

Architect
Hopkins Architects

Hopkins Directors
Sir Michael Hopkins, Andrew Barnett, Pamela Bate, Jonathan Knight,

Hopkins Project Director
Gary Clark

Hopkins Design Team
Wilson Au-Yeung, Luke Chandresinghe, Martyn Corner, Matthew Davies, Steve Jones, Margaret Leong, Arifa Salim, Andy Shaw, Jenny Stevens, Tim Whiteley

Project Manager
Bucknall Austin Limited

Structural Engineer
Arup

Main Contractor
Ashe Construction Ltd

Quantity Surveyor
Bucknall Austin Limited

The Wellcome Trust Gibbs Building, London
1999–2004

Client
The Wellcome Trust

Architect
Hopkins Architects

Hopkins Directors
Sir Michael Hopkins, William Taylor, Andrew Barnett, Pamela Bate, Michael Taylor, Simon Fraser

Hopkins Project Directors
Julie Gaulter, Tom Holdom

Hopkins Design Team
Wilson Au-Yeung, Martyn Corner, Alex Gino, Chris Gray, Steve Harris, Caroline Hislop, Annabel Hollick, Henry Kong, Nils Langer, Aurelie Lethu, Steve Mason, Emma Nsugbe, Aikari Paing, Andy Shaw, Alex Sykes, Angus Waddington, Tim Whiteley

Structural Engineer
WSP Consulting Engineers

Services Engineer
Cundall Johnston & Partners

Quantity Surveyor
Turner & Townsend

Project Manager
Mace Ltd

Construction Manager
Mace Ltd

Acoustician
Hann Tucker Associates

Information Technology Consultancy
Hurley Palmer Flatt

Artwork
Thomas Heatherwick Studio

Evelina Children's Hospital, London
1999–2005

Client
Guy's and St Thomas' Hospital NHS Foundation Trust
Guy's and St Thomas' Charity

Architect
Hopkins Architects

Hopkins Directors
Sir Michael Hopkins, William Taylor, Andrew

Barnett, Pamela Bate, James Greaves, Peter Romaniuk, Patrick Nee

Hopkins Project Directors
Ken Hood, Jan Mackie

Hopkins Design Team
Namit Agarwal, Sam Aldred, Jeannine Baker, Elizabeth Bartlett, Rory Campbell-Lange, Gary Collins, Martyn Corner, Chris Gray, Simon Goode, Alexandra Harris, Andrew Harrison, Phu Hoang, Aidan Hoggard, Yasuko Kobayashi, Steve Mason, Doron Meinhard, Amy Napier, Kelly Norris, Anastasia Rudenco, Alexandra Small, Jenny Stevens, Tom Stevens, Sonja Stoffels, Sadie Snelson, Paul Vick, Shyue-Jiun Woon, Louise Ward, Matt Williams

Structural Engineer
Buro Happold

Mechanical and Electrical Consultant
Hoare Lea and Partners

Main Contractor
Gleesons (Southern Construction Division)

Quantity Surveyor
David Langdon and Everest

National Tennis Centre, Roehampton, London
1999–2007

Client
The Lawn Tennis Association

Architect
Hopkins Architects

Hopkins Directors
Sir Michael Hopkins, William Taylor, Chris Bannister, Ernest Fasanya, Jonathan Knight, David Selby

Hopkins Project Directors
Sophy Twohig, Julie Gaultier

Hopkins Design Team
James Bichard, Kirsten Church, Claire Fleetwood, Chris Gray, Jorge Jover, Chikako Kanamoto, Carsten Kling, Yasuko Kobayashi, David Merks, Catherine Outram, Arifa Salim, Sumreen Salim, Cristina Segni, Andy Shaw, Jenny

Stevens, Sonya Stoffels, Paul Thomas, Jinbok Wee, Tony White

Structural Engineer
Ove Arup & Partners

Services Engineer
Ove Arup & Partners

Main Contractor
Buro 4 Project Services

Quantity Surveyor
Gardiner & Theobald

Planning Consultant
Rolf Judd Planning

Landscape Consultant
Broadway Malyan

Transport Consultant
Savell Bird and Axon

GEK-Terna Headquarters, Athens, Greece
2000–03

Client
GEK S A-TERNA S A

Architect
Hopkins Architects

Hopkins Directors
Sir Michael Hopkins, Simon Fraser

Hopkins Design Team
Andrew Ardill, Martyn Corner, Hiroaki Hoshino, Shigeru Hiraki, Vassiliki Kouvaki, Arifa Salim

Main Contractor
GEK S A-TERNA S A

Structural Engineer
P Madas & Associates

Service Engineers
HLMME

"Utopia" Broughton Hall, Yorkshire
2001–05

Client
Broughton Hall Business Park

Architect
Hopkins Architects

Hopkins Directors
Sir Michael Hopkins, David Selby

Hopkins Project Directors
Peter Mouncey, Tim Sloan

Hopkins Design Team
Jamie Brown, Carsten Cling, Federico Florena, Margaret Leong

Structural Engineer

Buro Happold

Services Engineer
Rural Solutions Ltd

Main Contractor
Broughton Hall Estate/Rural Solutions Ltd

Quantity Surveyor
Gardiner & Theobald

Landscape Architects
Dan Pearson

Shin-Marunouchi, Tokyo, Japan
2001–07

Client
Mitsubishi Jisho Sekkei

Architect
Hopkins Architects

Hopkins Directors
Sir Michael Hopkins, William Taylor, Simon Fraser

Hopkins Project Directors
Gary Clark, Jan Mackie, Tim Sloan

Hopkins Design Team
Andrew Ardill, Stephanie Gladbach, Paul Higginson, Shigeru Hiraki, Hiroaki Hoshino, Carolin Jacob, Carsten Kling, Stephen Luxford, Josuke Nagumo, Aikari Paing, Leonardo Pelleriti, Anthony Smith, Taro Tsuruta, Shyue-Jiun Woon

Co-architect & Engineers
Mitsubishi Jisho Sekkei

Structural Engineer
Expedition Engineering (competition phase only)

Services Engineer
Cundall Johnston and Partners (competition phase only)

Main Contractor
Takenaka Corporation

The New Science Building, Bryanston School, Blandford, Dorset
2002–07

Client
Bryanston School

Architect
Hopkins Architects

Hopkins Directors
Sir Michael Hopkins, Michael Taylor, Andrew Barnett

Hopkins Project Director
Sophy Twohig

Hopkins Design Team
Jennie Brown, Tim Coleridge, Emma Frater, Tom Jenkins, Kyle Konis, Oxana Krause, Andrew Stanforth, Jenny Stevens, Sarah Tassell

Structural Engineer
Buro Happold

Services Engineer
Cundall Johnston & Partners (CJP)

Main Contractor
Dean & Dyball Construction Limited

Quantity Surveyor
Turner Townsend

Royal Academy of Arts, London
2003

Client
Royal Academy of Arts

Architect
Hopkins Architects

Hopkins Directors
Sir Michael Hopkins, Lady Patricia Hopkins, David Selby

Hopkins Project Directors
Arif Mehmood, Michael Taylor

Hopkins Design Team
Jamie Brown, Martyn Corner, Alison Fisher, Chris Gray, Andrew Jordan, Carsten Kling, Maria Kramer, Margaret Leong, David Marks, James O'Leary, Catherine Outram, Hannah Wooler

Engineer
Alan Baxter Associates

Quantity Surveyor
Northcroft

Northern Arizona University Advance Research and Development Facility, Flagstaff, USA
2003–

Client
Northern Arizona University

Architect
Hopkins Architects

Hopkins Directors

Sir Michael Hopkins, William Taylor, Michael Taylor, Andrew Barnett

Hopkins Project Director
Gary Clark

Hopkins Design Team
Tom Jenkins, Henry Kong, Oxana Krause, Andrew Stanforth, Louise Ward

Associated Architect
Burns Wald-Hopkins Architects

Structural Engineer
Arup

Services Engineer
Arup

Lab Consultant
EarlWalls Associates

Main Contractor
Kitchells Construction Ltd

Quantity Surveyor
Kitchells Construction Ltd

Provincial Headquarter, Pisa, Italy
2003

Client
Province of Pisa

Architect
Hopkins Architects

Hopkins Directors
Sir Michael Hopkins, Simon Fraser, Michael Taylor

Hopkins Design Team
Laura Carrara-Cagni, Jan Mackie, Yosuke Nagumo, Andrew Ardill, Hiroaki Hoshino, Joe Bedford, Gabby Shawcross, Mark Tynan, Chris Gray, Jenny Stevens, Alex Whiteley

Alnwick Garden Pavilion, Northumberland
2003–06

Client
The Alnwick Garden Trust

Architect
Hopkins Architects

Hopkins Directors
Sir Michael Hopkins, Lady Patricia Hopkins, Pamela Bate, Jonathan Knight, William Taylor

Hopkins Project Director
Peter Mouncey

Hopkins Design Team
Kirsten Church, Clare Fleetwood, Paul Higginson,

Jorge Jover, Ines Marcelino, Amy Napier, Ben Thomas, Haseb Zada,

Structural Engineer
Buro Happold

Services Engineer
Battle McCarthy

Main Contractor
Sir Robert McAlpine

Quantity Surveyor
Summers Inman

Hälley VI, British Antarctic Survey
2005

Client
British Antarctic Survey

Architect
Hopkins Architects

Hopkins Directors
Sir Michael Hopkins, William Taylor, Michael Taylor

Hopkins Project Director
Tim Sloan

Hopkins Design Team
Martyn Corner, Alexandra Harris, Buddy Haward, Henry Kong, Oxana Krause, Anders Lendager, Mads Moller, Laura Rowley, Andrew Stanforth, Louise Ward

Structural & Civil Engineers
Expedition Engineering

Environmental Design
Atelier 10

Environmental Design Consultancy
HL Technik

Main Contractor
Morrisons Construction Services

Quantity Surveyor
Davis Langdon

Ambulatory Cancer Care Centre, University College London Hospitals
2005–

Client
University College London Hospitals

Architect
Hopkins Architects

Hopkins Directors
Sir Michael Hopkins, Andrew Barnett, William Taylor, Edward Williams

Hopkins Design Team
Simon Chenery, Hannah Heathcote, Paul Higginson, Andy Shaw, Andrew Stanforth, Ben Thomas, Laura Wilsdon, Sam White

Project Manager
Inventures

Structural Engineer
Waterman Partnership

Services Engineer
Hulley & Kirkwood

Quantity Surveyor
Turner & Townsend

Healthcare Planner
Tribal Secta

Chemistry Building, Princeton University, Princeton, USA
2005–

Client
Princeton University

Architect
Hopkins Architect

Hopkins Directors
Sir Michael Hopkins, Michael Taylor, William Taylor

Hopkins Design Team
Jennie Brown, Laura Gelso, Tony Ip, Henry Kong, Andrew Stanforth, Paul Thomas

Structural Engineer
ARUP

Services Engineer
ARUP

Main Contractor
Turner Construction

Quantity Surveyor
Hanscomb, Faith & Gould

The Kroon Building, School of Forestry and Environmental Studies, Yale University, New Haven, USA
2005–

Client
Yale School of Forestry and Environmental Studies

Architect
Hopkins Architects

Hopkins Directors
Sir Michael Hopkins, Michael Taylor

Hopkins Project Director
Sophy Twohig

Hopkins Design Team
Jennie Brown, Rose Evans, Edmund Fowles, Tom Jenkins, Henry Kong, Kyle Konis, Andrew Stanforth

Structural Engineer
Arup

Services Engineer
Arup

Sustainable Consultant
Atelier 10

Main Contractor
Turner Construction

Quantity Surveyor
Hanscomb Faithful & Gould

Photographic credits

Alinari, Florence p. 72 right
Dave Bower pp. 39, 45, 53, 54, 55, 56-57, 67, 68
Richard Bryant/Arcaid pp. 10, 40-41, 65, 69 bottom
Mike Cadwell p. 154
Martin Charles pp. 20 top, 59, 60, 63, 69 top, 73, 96, 98, 100, 101, 109
Peter Cook pp. 83, 85 top, 85 bottom
Nikos Daniilidis pp. 139, 141, 142 right
Richard Davies pp. 24, 43, 86, 87, 95, 102-103, 119, 123, 124, 125, 126, 127, 161, 165, 168 bottom, 170, 171, 203, 206 bottom, 217, 223, 249
Alan Delaney pp. 71, 75, 76-77
Mark Fiennes p. 79
Simon Fraser pp. 142 left, 143, 262 bottom right, 263 bottom left, 263 bottom right, 264 bottom left
Dennis Gilbert pp. 47, 48-49 top, 50-51, 107, 110, 111, 113, 114-115, 116, 117, 128, 189 top, 189 bottom, 197, 200, 201, 208, 218, 219, 220, 233, 234, 235, 236-237, 239, 241 top, 241 bottom
Nick Guttridge pp. 20 centro, 131, 133, 134, 135, 136-137
Martine Hamiliton Knight pp. 108 top left, 108 top right, 207, 210, 211, 212-213, 215
Chorley Handford p. 108 bottom
Paul Harmer/Building p. 89
Michael Hopkins p. 30 top
Hopkins Architects pp. 20 bottom, 145, 146-147, 224, 226-227, 227 top, 229 top, 229 bottom, 231 top, 231 bottom, 258, 259, 260, 263 top, 265, 270
Alastair Hunter pp. 80, 81
Keith Hunter pp. 181, 182-183 bottom, 184, 185
Nick Kane/Arcaid p. 104
Ken Kirkwood pp. 33, 36 top, 36 bottom, 37
Ian Lawson p. 205
Peter Mackinven pp. 22 bottom, 191, 193, 194, 195, 247
Melon Studio pp. 148, 149, 156
Simon Miles pp. 177, 178, 179 top, 179 bottom
Tom Miller pp. 192, 272
James Mortimer p. 31
Mandy Reynolds pp. 157, 159
Ianthe Ruthven pp. 243, 244 top, 244 bottom, 245
Timothy Soar pp. 90, 91, 151
Tim Street Porter p. 29
Paul Tyagi pp. 22 top, 162, 163, 168 top, 169, 173, 175, 251, 253, 254 top and bottom, 255, 256
University of Nottingham p. 206 top
Morley Von Sternberg pp. 24, 153, 155
Francis Ware p. 202
Antony Weller p. 122
Matthew Wienreb pp. 27, 30 bottom
Adam Wilson p. 187
Jonathan Youvens pp. 92-93